Lectures on
Elements
of
Business Logistics

E. GROSVENOR PLOWMAN

Visiting Professor of Business Logistics

Stanford University
GRADUATE SCHOOL OF BUSINESS

1964

TO
GENIFRED

STANFORD TRANSPORTATION SERIES

Published by the Graduate School of Business

FOREWORD

Grosvenor Plowman has combined in an unusual and effective way an academic and a business career. Starting with a B.S. degree from Dartmouth and a year at the Harvard Business School, he went on to obtain a Ph.D. from the University of Chicago. He was an effective teacher of economics at the Massachusetts Institute of Technology, Boston University, and the University of Denver. While in Colorado, he began to do some consulting work for the Colorado Iron and Fuel Company at Pueblo. He was so effective that he subsequently gave up his teaching to become the traffic manager for that organization.

After seven years with this company, he accepted the invitation of the U.S. Steel Corporation to become its Vice President of Traffic. During this period he not only wrote many an article, but produced his "Business Organization and Management" with Elmore Petersen. The quality and success of this work are attested by the fact that twenty-one years later it is in its fifth edition. Throughout his business career Grosvenor Plowman has continued to be a thoughtful student of business administration. He is the author of many articles in that broad field and he has been often sought as a speaker.

He has been one of the real leaders in traffic and transportation, focusing much of his attention on the raising of the standards and the morale of those engaged therein. He has been particularly active in the National Defense Transportation Association where he has been concerned with preparing civilians in the transportation field for wartime emergencies. He has been a leader in the American Society of Traffic and Transportation, whose major purpose is to raise standards in the field. He has been more than a "founder member"; in a true sense he was one of the few real founders of the organization, for he was among those that conceived it and got it under way.

Grosvenor has combined to an unusual degree a vast storehouse of practical experience and an avid thirst for knowledge. He has been interested in a wide variety of innovations including an improved draw bar for freight cars, more efficient motive equipment, and the integral train. He was one of the first advocates of more research in the transportation industry, making use of the latest management tools and techniques. As chairman of the Research Committee of the Transportation Association of America he has focused on the research needs of the industry, and he has worked increasingly to fill those research gaps and to encourage others to do likewise.

GEORGE P. BAKER

Harvard University
April 8, 1963

PREFACE

During the quarter of a century since 1937 a new kind of integration of business activity has been evolving. It is in addition to and different from the horizontal integration that results in one retail store proliferating into a chain of like commercial enterprises. It differs also from the vertical integration that links an automobile assembly plant backwards to include parts manufacturing and forward to include the function of wholesale distribution of cars to retailers. This third kind of integration is of total or overall responsibility for the creation of usefulness for the customer.

In terms used by economists, the creation of *form utility* by making a product must be accompanied by creation of *location utility* by getting the product to a user and *timeliness utility* by getting it to him when he needs it, neither too long before nor too long afterward. In terms used by some business consultants and authors, the new frontier for the pioneers who seek and find important cost reductions is in the area of physical distribution, for example, getting a food product from the end of the factory assembly line to the customer's breakfast table. In this area efficient conveyor belts and containers are still intermingled with large amounts of the sweaty kind of hand labor. Here the rapid and reliable performance of one operation tends to be nullified by the different work conditions of another related activity. At ocean ports, for example, longshoremen unloading a vessel often have to wait for the "hook"; then, in turn, the crane has to wait for them.

The term used herein to describe this third type of integration is business logistics. Authority for such use is found in the term logistics in military management, meaning all the details of matériel procurement and supply and resupply that, taken as a whole, make it possible for an army to march and fight. Business logistics includes all activities directly related to manufacturing and distribution other than making the product or the commercial service and selling it. Thus defined and limited it is a staff activity that facilitates making and selling.

Business logistics involves acceptance of responsibility for the decisions and actions of insiders and outsiders, that is, of employees and non-employees. The common carrier by rail or truck or barge or air is an example of a separate enterprise that often fills a vital role in getting a product to a customer where and when he wants it. This acceptance of total or overall responsibility creates the third kind of integration, that is, *logistical integration.*

This book is based on a similarly titled mimeographed text used in the Transportation Management Program in 1962. Most of the material consisted originally of excerpts from speeches made during the twenty years beginning in 1944.

Grateful acknowledgment is made to Dr. Beatrice Aitchison for her assistance in rearranging and coordinating the 1963 material into book form. Dr. Karl Ruppenthal and Dr. Gayton Germane have been stimulating and constructive readers of the manuscript. The thoughts herein expressed are my own, but grateful acknowledgment is due the many friends who have helped in their shaping and evolution. Particular recognition is due to the late Dr. G. Lloyd Wilson who, for more than a decade, was my counsellor and teacher. It is scarcely necessary to add that the point of view of the author is derived from years of service in small and large manufacturing enterprises.

Miss Gale McLain who typed the manuscript twice from exceedingly rough notes also deserves special thanks which are hereby tendered.

E. GROSVENOR PLOWMAN

Portland, Maine
February 23, 1963

Editor's Note

In every human endeavor there have been outstanding men whose great vision has enabled them to understand important problems and whose dedication has impelled them to do something about them. There are great men of science, masters in the arts, wizards in production, and statesmen in business. Grosvenor Plowman is one of those giants.

Long before most people recognized the importance of transportation to the economy, he was writing profusely on that importance. Long before most businessmen recognized the importance of industrial traffic management, he was speaking on that subject throughout the land. Certainly no man has understood more clearly the fact that our economy cannot exist without transportation and that it must be efficient and profitable to survive. He has made no secret of his belief that if private enterprise fails in the transportation industry, and the government enters by that default, the death knell may be sounded for private enterprise as we know it in this country.

The Plowman Lectures on Business Logistics represent the work of many years. Many of the themes contained therein have been the subject of previous talks. The Lectures were first delivered in their entirety at Stanford in 1962 when Dr. Plowman graciously consented to teach in the Transportation Management Program. He delivered them again at Stanford in 1963. We think that they are so provocative and so important that they deserve a much wider adherence than any classroom can provide.

KARL M. RUPPENTHAL

Stanford, California
July 20, 1963

ix

CONTENTS

Chapter I

BUSINESS LOGISTICS REVIEWED

More than 2000 years ago Greek thinkers were using two closely related words that have become in our language *logic* and *logistic*. As used in Ancient Greece by scholars such as Aristotle or Euclid, they applied to two different methods of reasoning or thinking. These meanings are still applicable today.

According to the dictionary, *logic* is the science of correct reasoning, as by deduction or analogy. *Logistic* is the science of correct reasoning by calculation, that is, by means of mathematics. To restate, *logic* means thinking, using words and sentences as the device or technique. *Logistic* also means thinking, using the symbols or numbers of mathematics as its device or technique.

Logistics, a plural word derived from *logistic* means, in military science, the planning and handling and implementation of personnel, also the related materiel, facilities, and other factors. Thus *logistics* means the application of reasoning, especially mathematical analysis and synthesis, to the complex and inter-related problems of coordinating manpower and supplies and barracks. Military *logistics* is a major factor in making it possible for an army to march and fight and win its battles. As thus defined *military logistics* includes the inter-related and largely mathematical procedures, and the resulting coordinating decisions.

What is business logistics?

The *logistics* concept, as applied to business management, similarly is a reasoning process using and aided by mathemat-

1

ics. Its aim is to achieve optimum coordination of the inbound material movements, raw materials storage, work-in-process handling, and of the outbound packaging, warehousing of finished products, and movement of finished products to the customer. Consideration of location of raw material origins, producing plants, warehouses and consumer destinations also is inherent in business *logistics,* since each decision involves a choice between what can be made available by a change in the arrangement or location of the numerous factors. Selection of the best from among the numerous choices and combinations of choices is facilitated and often is possible only through the use of mathematical techniques. Thus *business logistics,* like its military counterpart consists of both mathematical procedures and coordinated decisions.

WHAT BUSINESS LOGISTICS INCLUDES

The following check-list is presented at this point to show the complexity of the inter-relations of the numerous choice-factors that facilitate production and marketing. This check-list is intentionally not complete, thus emphasizing that new factors arise and old factors change in importance. It has been arranged in sequential fashion in and out of a typical factory to show the inter-twining of the three "economic utilities" or types of "value creation." These are change of form of some material, change of its location by means of transportation, and making it available when needed, which is also often dependent on transportation. These are commonly called *form, place,* and *time* utilities.

Since business logistics deals primarily with facilitation and coordination of production and marketing, that is, with creation of "place" and "time" utility, the role of transportation is pervasive and vital. Hence much of this text will be directly concerned with the problems and opportunities contributed by modern mechanized transportation to the logistics area of business enterprise.

A. *The pre-production or inbound choice factors*

1. *Procurement or production of raw materials or components that enter into the finished product at a factory (i.e., a place where form utility is created).* These initial procurement or production decisions are influenced by or even determined by their possible alternative locations in relation to the location of the factory.

2. *Coordination of the efficient rate of production of the raw material or component and the efficient rate of scheduled arrival at the factory to achieve optimum unit cost and adequate protection against interruptions.*

   a. Raw material or component output rates may be subject to predictable variations, such as seasonal effects, requiring origin reserve storage with resulting stocking and destocking costs. This is true of component materials or parts whether "self-produced" or purchased "from outside."

   b. The transportation loading device usually must be operated at a rate different from the output rate, making loading of current production without going through the stockpile impossible without additional transportation cost, such as cars waiting to be loaded.

3. *Scheduling production, over-all and in detail, of the finished products* so as to achieve optimum conditions in procurement of inbound materials and in coordination of rates of production and outbound shipment with the arrival of inbound materials; so as to achieve minimum work-in-process inventories combined with minimum customer dissatisfaction with quality failures and broken delivery promises; and to achieve planned maintenance of optimum in-

ventories of finished merchandise in one or several warehouses.

B. *The post-production or outbound choice factors*

1. *Processing the order, including choice between alternative locations of production if available, and handling of paper work so as to avoid its interference with the delivery promise.* This processing function must be intertwined with the production scheduling decisions outlined above.

2. *Packaging, including assembly into groups, for example, assembly of items in a box or crate or lift for ease of shipment, also initial warehousing at or near the production location if required.*

3. *Loading in transportation equipment (freight car, truck, barge, vessel, or aircraft) including compliance with dunnage and securement requirements, shipping and unloading.* This activity is transportation as it is commonly thought of. It involves selection of carrier, consideration of cost and service, and the influence on future choices of what has happened in the past. This concept of "transportation" is gradually being broadened into inclusion of all factors that make up what is called "total cost." Total cost includes *all costs related to movement* between the machine where the product is finished and the unloading platform at the customer's plant or store.

4. *Field warehousing at or near the anticipated "purchaser's location."* This usually involves choice of the optimum location; use of efficient unloading, break-bulk and storing methods; also equipment facilities, when required for minor processing such as cutting to lengths desired by the customer; and efficient methods for loading, shipment and delivery of finished products as ordered by the customer.

Field warehousing does not take place when shipments can be advantageously made direct from factory to purchaser. Often delivery from a field warehouse is made by an employee who has multiple skills, i.e., the driver-salesman.

The staff nature of business logistics

The facilitative functions which make up business logistics have two common characteristics. Each is a staff activity, and each results in a "transportation-choice" decision.

Staff activities may be divided into two general types, advisory and supportive. Advisory staff activities involve no decision-making, only advice, as when a lawyer suggests to his client clauses that should be in a proposed contract. Supportive staff executives and employees do make decisions within their own area. But supportive decisions are made only to aid the factory to make finished products and to help the sales force to sell them to customers.

The supportive functional activities of the above-described check list may be organized into departments or sub-departments in any one of three different ways. The particular choice determines who is to be the logistician. The three alternatives

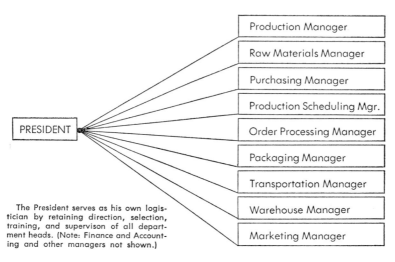

PRESIDENT

Production Manager
Raw Materials Manager
Purchasing Manager
Production Scheduling Mgr.
Order Processing Manager
Packaging Manager
Transportation Manager
Warehouse Manager
Marketing Manager

The President serves as his own logistician by retaining direction, selection, training, and supervison of all department heads. (Note: Finance and Accounting and other managers not shown.)

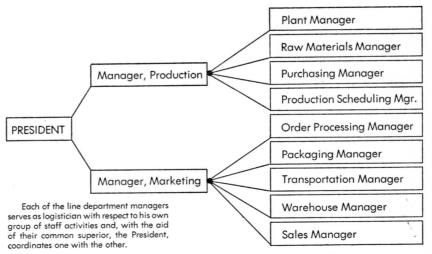

Each of the line department managers serves as logistician with respect to his own group of staff activities and, with the aid of their common superior, the President, coordinates one with the other.

may be described as the "flattened," the "normal" and the "recentralized" types of organization structure.

The "flattened" organization structure develops when the company top executive maintains direct contact with each line and each staff department manager.

The "normal" organization structure develops when the supportive functions are grouped, in appropriate manner, under the heads of the making and selling line departments.

The "recentralized" organization structure develops when the supportive functions are grouped together under their own manager, who is the logistician. This resembles the military type of logistics or "service of supply" organization. It relieves both the President and the two line department heads of many of their logistics coordination problems, since they become the task of the logistician. Being a staff manager, the logistician is subordinate to the two line department executives. His task is to aid them in their work.

Choice of the most appropriate organization structure for the logistics function or activity depends, in part, on the size and resulting complexity of a business enterprise. It also depends on the relative importance of the directly related costs that must be incurred. Examples of such costs are storage of

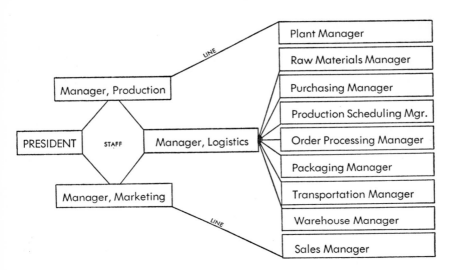

raw materials, procurement and transportation of "inbound materials" including purchased items, "work-in-process" handling, packaging and protection of finished products by storage or other means, transportation to the customer with or without additional warehousing, and "paperwork" including order processing and production scheduling. In some enterprises these costs are minor. In others these expenses, that do not either create the product or sell it, may amount to a substantial portion of the price paid by the customer. This is often true, for example, of food products prepared for the user by canning or packaging.

The logistics kind of reasoning seeks, by calculation and comparison of the various possibilities, to find the best arrangement of the supportive activities that add to unit cost but do not change the product itself. Electronic data processing has increased the usefulness of this mathematics-using technique, hence has made it more important in business management. By itself, EDP may appear to have added itself to cost; however, if properly developed by "systems analysis" and the like, EDP can open new vistas of information worth many times its cost.

The transportation element in logistics

The military adage that "an army travels on its stomach" emphasizes the importance of mechanized transportation as a major factor in modern military logistics. Similarly, in business logistics, transportation is a major cost factor. At least as important is the effect of the transportation choice upon all other elements of cost. Erratic delivery of inbound materials increases inventories and may even shut down plants. Delivery of a damaged product to a customer may lose his future patronage. The following reviews of contemporary nineteenth century appraisals of the role of transportation will bring its relation to business logistics into sharper focus.

AMERICA'S INDUSTRIAL PROGRESS (AS OF 1870)

The book containing this description of transportation almost 100 years ago is entitled "One Hundred Years' Progress of the United States," with an appendix entitled "One Hundred Years' Progress in the Future." The title refers to the century of progress from 1770, just before the Revolutionary War, to 1870, just after the War between the States. The authors of this well-written and illustrated parlor book were so sure of their own judgment that they also included a lengthy final appendix telling their readers all about the United States one hundred years later, that is, in 1970.[1]

Of course, writing almost a century ago, they knew that the wonderful machines that had transformed America were driven by means of steam. As they put it, "improvements in the steam engine are being made every day and we believe that the consumption of only one pound of coal to the horsepower will soon be accomplished. In view of all the facts that have been adduced to prove that the steam engine is the best of all motors," they continue, "can it be possible that there are still

---

[1] One Hundred Years Progress, including sections on Steam Engine by J. C. Merriam, on Improvements in the Means of Travel and Transportation by T. P. Kettel, and Appendix by L. P. Brockett; L. Stebbins, Publisher; Hartford, Conn., 1871, p. 264.

those who are skeptical on the subject of its utility? Alas, Yes! You will find them among those who object to the use of steam in our streets to replace the horse cars."

Beginnings of steam-powered navigation

Their story of 100 years of American progress, up to the year 1870, included the sudden and dramatic invention and development of the steamboat, the steam locomotive and its rail track, and the macadam or gravel surface road. The latter is appropriately named for Mr. McAdam, the Scot who invented this highway improvement about 1820. The book describes these developments in great detail, stating that "of all marvels that have marked the century . . . the development of the means of locomotion and transportation are among the most wonderful."[2] Of course, speed was the marvelous part but reduction in cost of freight transportation was more noteworthy. As to speed, they had lots to talk about. In 1811, they told their amazed readers, the world's first commercial steamer, the Clermont, made its trip from New York up the Hudson to Albany at four miles per hour, in one and one-half days. In 1870, this same trip *was being made at 21 miles per hour,* taking only 7 hours.[3]

The use of steamboats on the vast Mississippi River system was one of the great steps forward in navigation during America's first 100 years of progress. About 1825, "a bold merchant predicted that the rate of freight between New Orleans and St. Louis would fall to $3.50 per 100 pounds [or $70.00 per ton for the 1,300-mile river trip], but he was regarded as visionary." . . . "His sanguine nature would probably have been surprised," our authors continue, "could the veil of time have been so lifted as to permit him to see ahead to the boats of the present day making money at 40 cents per 100 pounds, and carrying it in three days instead of 25."[4] Our visionary merchant of 1825 would have been even more amazed if he could

---

[2] *Ibid.,* p. 173.
[3] *Ibid.,* p. 180.
[4] *Ibid.,* p. 181.

have seen a group of 15 or 20 loaded barges leaving New Orleans or St. Louis today, pushed by a diesel vessel, its cargo paying substantially less than $8.00 per ton when the present-day charges are converted back into the value of the money in 1860.

The Erie Canal, completed in 1825, was equally dramatic in its effect on freight cost. "A single horse can draw upon a good road a ton at a speed of 2½ or 3 miles per hour, and can draw as easily 70 tons upon a canal at the same speed. The difference in cost is immense. Instead of 24 cents a ton for one mile land carriage, the Erie Canal charges 6 mills per ton per mile . . . [plus] the state tolls. . . . Before the canal was built, the expense of transportation from Buffalo to New York was $100 per ton and the time 20 days. . . . When the canal was opened, the freight went down to $14 per ton, more or less, according to the character of the freight. This has gradually been reduced, and in 1850, when the railroads for the first time were allowed to carry freight (in direct competition with the Erie Canal), it was $3 to $7 from Buffalo to New York."[5]

These authors, writing in 1870, also forecast great improvement in ocean navigation. . . . "The sea-going [iron hull] vessel, propelled by some efficient motive power—steam, or hot or condensed air, solar heat or some application of electricity, will sail daily by scores from all our principal ports . . . and, either by reducing the friction or increasing the power or rapidity of action of their propellers, they will reduce the time of the trip across the Atlantic to four days, and that across the Pacific to nine or ten."[6]

Beginnings of the steam-powered railroads

Now let's see what 1870 knew about railroads. "The excitement in relation to canals and steamboats was at its zenith," these authors stated, "when the air began to be filled with rumors of the new application of steam to land carriages and to

---

[5] *Ibid.,* p. 186.
[6] *Ibid.,* p. 483.

railroads. There were many inventions and patents at home and abroad in relation to carriages propelled by steam, but these seem never to have attained much success, although attempts to perfect them are still made with great perseverance. On the other hand, the use of railroads from small beginnings has reached a magnitude which overshadows the wildest imagining of the most sanguine."[7] "It is to be remarked," they continued, "that the national *government expended*, . . . largely in the construction of highways, the clearing out of rivers, and the improvement of harbors.[8] . . . The railroads of the country have been, as a whole, built . . . by corporations. . . . The great advantage of railroads is that they practically diminish distances between places in proportion to the speed attained."[9]

"Within a few years past," it was further stated, "it has been found that steel rails possess great advantages over iron. . . . The most important single article of freight transported by the railroads is coal."[10] "There have recently been introduced on the long lines sleeping cars wherein the passenger takes his natural rest while the iron horse is whirling him towards his destination at the rate of 30 miles an hour."[11]

This book reviewing the first century of American Progress, emphasized the role of the great common carrier of that era, the railroad, in contributing to the public welfare by fostering the already amazing growth of our country. The authors linked dynamic transportation expansion with similar expansion of all other factors, such as capital formation, land values, industrial growth, and population growth.

By 1970 suburban commutation would be, they believed, by means of "elegant, well-lighted cars, which are ventilated, as well as propelled, by compressed air, and are driven at a

---

[7] *Ibid.,* p. 191.
[8] *Ibid.,* p. 193.
[9] *Ibid.,* p. 193.
[10] *Ibid.,* p. 220.
[11] *Ibid.,* p. 221.

speed of about 120 miles an hour. . . . City streets will be broad and paved in the carriage way with a slightly elastic composition . . . sidewalks covered with an artificial stone."[12] However, the authors admit that "We cannot tell how soon the steam locomotive or some new motor may take the place of the horse before our pleasure carriage. . . . The uncertainty," the authors continue their forecast of 1970, "in regard to our means of locomotion in the future makes an estimate of the production somewhat difficult; the steam locomotive may then be entirely superseded; the ponderous railroad car may be replaced by a carriage combining extreme lightness and strength and this may be propelled under the earth in tubes, or above it on elevated railways, or through the air; heavy freight may be sent to its destination, in spheres."[13]

AMERICA'S INDUSTRIAL PROGRESS (AS OF 1888)

It is often said that the problems of today grow out of the facts of yesterday. With this in mind, perspective as to business logistics problems will be aided by a brief look through the eyes of a great American steel maker, Andrew Carnegie. Before he became one of the world's greatest steel executives and one of the world's wisest philanthropists, he had had a youthful decade of employment as a railroad executive. Carnegie went to work for the Pennsylvania Railroad in 1853, the year its rails reached Pittsburgh from Philadelphia. In 1859 he was made General Manager of the Pittsburgh Region of this railroad at the remarkable age of twenty-four. Three years later, during the War between the States, he served President Lincoln in a position that today would probably be called Director of Military Transportation.

At the height of his career three-fourths of a century ago, Andrew Carnegie wrote Triumphant Democracy, with subtitle Fifty Years March of the Republic.

A major purpose of this writing project was to explain to or

---

[12] *Ibid.,* p. 523.
[13] *Ibid.,* p. 493.

perhaps astonish his English and Scotch friends, many of whom looked with prejudice and even contempt upon America.[14]

Carnegie's views on the railroads

Our interest in Carnegie's book is that in it he surveys and praises the large and small private enterprises engaged in transportation of his day as a keystone of American economic growth and prosperity during the half century ending in 1888.

"It is usual to speak of the United States as without commerce . . . " Carnegie wrote in 1888, because "the tendency is to limit the term commerce to the carriage of merchandise to and from other countries[15] . . . America has no business with ocean navigation till her continent is filled," he believed,[16] and he went on to state that the "American coasting tonnage alone more than doubles the entire foreign traffic, . . . while the domestic commerce by rail is reported as 291,000,000 tons and by steamers on lakes and rivers as 25,500,000 tons. Thus it appears that our internal commerce, of which so little is heard, is more than twenty times greater than the foreign trade."[17] "The American railway system, starting 55 years ago at nothing," he continued, "has reached, in 1885, 128,000 miles of line. The whole of Europe has not so many [miles]." Carnegie commented that "consolidation into . . . a few organizations seems the inevitable tendency. The saving and efficiency thus effected . . . are so manifestly great that nothing can prevent these consolidations."[18]

He concluded by pointing out that "In no other country is travel so comfortable and luxurious. For this we are chiefly indebted to a remarkable American invention, the sleeping car."[19] . . . However, despite this praise and looking into the future, Carnegie added this prophecy. "If ever aerial naviga-

---

[14] Triumphant Democracy, by Andrew Carnegie; Sampson, Low, London 1888, p. 47.
[15] Ibid., p. 188.
[16] Ibid., p. 189.
[17] Ibid., p. 190.
[18] Ibid., p. 205.
[19] Ibid., pp. 205–6.

tion becomes practicable it will like railways attain its highest development in America; for there men's lives are too full of activity to permit lounging in parlor cars drawn wearily by a locomotive at only 40 miles an hour when it is possible for men to soar through the air and outstrip their own symbolic eagle in its flight."[20]

Carnegie's views on water-borne commerce

Turning to the subject of vessel and barge transportation, he wrote that America's inland seas, containing one-third of all the fresh water in the world, and her great rivers lay ready at hand awaiting only the application of steam to vessels to render them magnificent highways.[21] "These great natural waterways have been supplemented and connected with each other by artificial canals."[22]

"The traffic floated upon these Western rivers will surprise many." added Carnegie. "Take the Ohio, for instance; a competent authority has stated that the total of its trade from its head at Pittsburgh to its mouth at New Cairo, about a thousand miles, exceeded in 1874 $800,000,000. . . . Coal, coke and other bulky articles are transported at the rate of one-twentieth of a cent, . . . per ton per mile. This is made possible by means of barges, many of which are lashed together, and pushed ahead by a steam tug."[23]

Carnegie's views on oil and gas pipelines

Carnegie saw that petroleum and natural gas were becoming important new industries.

"Seven years ago a company was drilling for petroleum at Murrysville, near Pittsburgh. A depth of 1,320 feet had been reached when the drills were thrown high into the air . . . by a tremendous explosion of gas. . . . Thinking it was but a temporary outburst preceding the oil, men allowed this valuable fuel to waste for five years. . . . A company was formed

[20] *Ibid.*, p. 208.
[21] *Ibid.*, p. 208.
[22] *Ibid.*, p. 210.
[23] *Ibid.*, p. 214.

to (conduct the gas in pipes) under the boilers of iron works, where it burned without a particle of smoke. . . . Numerous lines of pipes, aggregating 60 miles, now convey the gas from the wells to [Pittsburgh]. . . . Private residences in Pittsburgh are supplied with natural gas, and all heating and cooking are done with this cheap fuel. Already 10,000 tons of coal per day are displaced by it."[24]

Carnegie continued,

"An oil property, Storey Farms, Oil Creek, with which I was intimately connected, has a remarkable history. When about twenty-two years ago, in company with some friends, I first visited this famous well, the oil was running into . . . flat-bottomed scows . . . to be floated down to the Allegheny River upon an agreed-upon day each week, when the creek was flooded by means of a temporary dam."[25]

"So great was the yield of oil in this district that in two years oil became almost valueless, often selling in bulk as low as 30 cents per barrel. . . . But as new uses were found for the oil, prices rose again, and to remove the difficulty of high freights, pipes were laid . . . to the seaboard, a distance of about 300 miles. Through these pipes, of which 6,200 miles have been laid, the oil is now pumped from 2,100 wells. It costs only 10 cents to pump a barrel of oil to the Atlantic."[26]

Defense transportation was apparently purposely neglected by Carnegie. This was not due to lack of understanding, since he himself had had Civil War defense transportation experience, both on the Pennsylvania Railroad and in the government in Washington. His failure to discuss the subject probably reflected his belief that the United States should remain demobilized and almost undefended as it had become shortly after the end of the Civil War. He hoped that America would never again be required to build up a powerful military establishment. He thought and hoped that our example would be followed by the nations of Europe. Carnegie died in 1919, after we had

---

[24] *Ibid.*, pp. 168–69.
[25] *Ibid.*, pp. 170–71.
[26] *Ibid.*, pp. 171–72.

entered World War I, so he must have been sad and disillusioned on this subject. Today the United States must maintain adequate military strength. It follows, therefore, that the necessary defense and emergency transportation control procedures to assure an ample supply of specialized military transportation capability must be at all times in a state of readiness.

It is doubtful that Andrew Carnegie, extolling the march of economic progress in the United States, knew that he was recording the end of an era for competitive private enterprise transportation. 1888 was the first full year of operation of the Interstate Commerce Commission, which had been established by Congress in 1887 to regulate interstate railroad transportation. Carnegie does not mention this event in his book, probably because he had not at that time decided whether federal regulation of transportation would prove to be good or bad, important or unimportant.

THE NECESSITY FOR BUSINESS LOGISTICS

The year 1887 must be accepted as a turning point in the development of business logistics, because there was then added the factor of Federal regulation of transportation.

Business logistics, as a management technique, looks at transportation through the eyes of a user. The total cost concept links all the *facilitating or supportive functions* that aid in production and sale. This concept is important only if it is useful. If, as some pessimists believe, business enterprises must, in the future, create much of their own transportation, the regulated common carriers whose business activity is to supply transportation will be reduced in importance and may even disappear. If common carrier railroads, truckers, barge and vessel operators, air carriers and pipeline enterpises all become unimportant or even disappear, present-day regulation will also become less important. However, this will not reduce the significance of 1887 as a turning point. Federal regulation began in 1887 in response to the fact that mechanized transportation had by then become nationwide and universally used.

Of course since then the national system has constantly expanded, both in variety of modal networks and in geographical coverage. Then as today, transportation was and is the movement of persons or property by any mode or combination of modes, where and when desired by the user, by means of energy mechanically converted into motion. Being power-driven, being inter-connected, being needed and used by everyone are the basic facts that have caused transportation to become a national problem. Establishment of the Interstate Commerce Commission in 1887 was the first major recognition of the need for national policies and actions.

The total cost concept of business logistics is that the sum of all the costs incurred in creating *place* and *time* utilities must be as low as possible consistent with creation of *form* utility. All the costs incurred that do not change the product, that do not manufacture it into saleable form, must be so coordinated and managed as to be at the lowest optimum level. Transportation is one of these costs. It is affected by Government policies and actions. However, Government policies and actions with respect to transportation may or may not be pertinent to or be related to private enterprise logistical goals. The commuter problem in large cities, for example, has many facets quite unrelated to business logistics. This difference in point of view is another reason for considering 1887 an important turning point.

Logistical decisions are reasoned, not habitual

This book deals primarily with the logistics aspects of transportation, but always from the *business-enterprise-as-a-user* point of view. The result is to consider all business logistics factors as if dependent upon transportation. Admittedly, this is over-emphasis. However, it is justified by the central fact that neither "inbound assembly" of materials needed for production, nor "outbound delivery" of finished articles to customers can be accomplished without use of modern, mechanized modes or kinds of transportation.

Logistical decisions of users may be observed to be the result both of reasoning and of habitual behavior patterns. Since the meaning of the term logistics includes the concept of use of mathematical reasoning, it follows that "habit patterns" may or may not result in defensible decisions.

Assuming, for example, that a typical business enterprise had to use common carrier railroads for its inbound raw materials and its outbound finished products, its freedom of choice might be between four competing carriers. Analogous to this is the plight of a five-year-old boy, offered his choice of one of four identically wrapped pieces of candy. His random choice will be determined by some external factor. He will pick the nearest one, or the one that a ray of sunshine happens to illuminate. This random method of choice is not very different from adult routing of freight when the decision is made because the solicitor is a "nice guy" or because he always offers a fine cigar. Repetition, both in the case of the boy and the adult, created a habit pattern that cannot be defended by appeal to reason. This random choice method of selecting transportation is still common.

Before 1887, government regulation intruded only slightly into user decision-making. Generally speaking, the company president was the concern's logistician, as well as its commander-in-chief. He encouraged the common carrier railroads to extend across the continent, because each extension increased the area from which his enterprise could draw inbound materials, and to which he could sell finished products. Using logistics as an important way of stimulating company growth was the keynote before 1887. Today logistics is again a key factor in assuring company growth or even survival, since its goal is to find the most favorable arrangement of all of the economic conditions, on both the inbound and outbound side of the production process. Logistics decisions also have become inter-twined with government decisions that affect both carriers and users. Thus user behavior may be forecast to become more logistical and less habitual. Hence today, as before 1887, logistics has a major role.

Line executives are a happily blessed race who radiate confidence and power. They stride confidently. They can develop a new pathway to greater profits merely by using decisive words and gestures. However, each line executive usually has one or more logisticians riding on his back. He knows that, at any moment, the logisticians may lean forward and whisper, "No, you can't do that." (An anonymous comment attributed to a military logistics officer.)

Chapter II

TRANSPORTATION VARIETY IS STILL INCREASING

In 1887 when the Interstate Commerce Commission became the first Federal regulatory agency, it must have seemed to many students of the transportation factor in business logistics that the railroads had become and would remain the dominant mode of transportation. All other kinds of mechanized transport might be confined by the impact of regulation of railroads to supplemental roles, such as local cartage of freight to and from railroad stations. In fact, as we know, this did not happen. Instead, beginning with pipelines and inland navigation, each mode became relatively independent of the railroads and developed its own nationwide network of interconnected routes. Today there is no dominant mode or kind of transportation, either regionally or nationally.

Efficient mechanized handling of both bulk and packaged freight into and out of storage and between carriers at transfer points also has developed. This makes possible low cost use of and satisfactory service on inter-modal routes. Containerization, especially when the container is a truck trailer body, has facilitated the forwarder and express modes of transportation of small packages. Thus the Federal government as a major shipper of mail and defense-related freight, can and does route its loaded containers via more than one mode—for example, truck-ocean. Private transporters of their own freight also find it advantageous to route their own trucks on railroad flat cars between origin and destination cities. Thus a new kind of supplementation of one mode by another has developed, but without destroying the independence of each mode.

21

This new co-mingling of the different kinds of transportation is important to the business logistician. It opens up new opportunities and additional alternative choices to the user, often with either cost or service advantages.

Transportation has been evolving for centuries

The slightly egg-shaped planet on which we live, less than 25,000 miles in circumference, was regarded by all primitive peoples as almost limitless in extent. This idea was well-founded since for centuries the highest average speed of traversing its surface was about five miles per hour, or about 50 to 100 miles per 24-hour day. Today commercial airplanes speed at 300 to 600 miles per hour, and the entire globe can be circled by a thrill-seeking passenger comfortably in less than a week. The common remark is that our world has shrunk. Truly, modern power-driven mechanized transportation has had the effect of making our terrestrial globe seem to be a smaller, if not a better place to live.

When Rome reigned over the Mediterranean shores 2000 years ago, there were also relatively advanced civilizations occupying the Indian peninsula and central China. These three widely separated centers of civilization of the ancient world engaged in internal trade and in foreign trade with each other. The sailing vessel, the first transportation device that enlisted other than human or animal power, evolved during the Roman era to relatively large size and efficiency. In the Mediterranean, Roman ships hugged the shore line for navigation reasons and protection from storms. They brought to the Italian "boot" the Egyptian grain needed to feed Rome's idle soldiers and trouble-making loafers.

The Romans also modernized and restored the still more ancient first Suez Canal. By about A.D. 100 this had become the major connecting link between Asia and Europe, a position it held until it again fell into disuse several centuries later. Between the Red Sea terminus of the Suez Canal and India, Roman sailing vessels learned how to use the monsoon winds and made a round voyage in about a year. Thus twenty centuries ago trade, using the most modern mass transportation device of the time—sail-propelled vessels—was already fulfilling its role of exchanging the surplus wealth of one region or nation for the equally valuable but different surplus of other regions or nations.

For more than fifteen hundred years after the era of the twelve Caesars there were only minor improvements in sailing vessels, roads, and in animal-drawn vehicles. Transportation continued to require the sweaty cooperation of men and horses or oxen on land, and of men and the natural forces of wind, tide and current on water.

One hundred years before the application of steam power to any form of transportation the first successful steam engine had been invented and used in England. The Newcomen coal mine pumping engine of 1705 was followed by the improved Watt engine in 1769. From then on, numerous inventive minds tackled the problem of installing a practicable steam engine in a ship. Half a dozen attempts to power a vessel failed. The engine wouldn't work reliably. The method of propelling the vessel was ineffective. Most important of all, the public regarded the devices as unsafe novelties and did not patronize them.

1807: The first successful steamboat

In 1802 Robert Fulton and Robert Livingston became partners in a joint venture to build a steamboat to be operated on the Hudson River. Fulton was to supply the inventive know-how. Livingston was to supply the money and the market. To guarantee the latter he obtained an exclusive franchise to operate steam-powered vessels between New York City and Albany. At that time the Hudson was crowded with small sailing vessels, called sloops, providing transportation for people and freight between the eastern seacoast and "the West," a term that then meant western New York state and the Ohio country.

In 1807 The Clermont made its successful trial trips, and thereafter served for years as part of a profitable steamboat operation of common carrier type on the New York to Albany route. Traffic developed and additional Hudson River boats were built. This prototype success was copied all over the world, first on inland rivers, such as the Ohio and Mississippi, and then on the ocean.

1830: The first successful railroad

Steam-powered railroads followed shortly after the steamboat era began in 1807. George Stephenson dominates the story of development, beginning in 1814 when he constructed and placed in operation a tiny steam-powered locomotive to haul coal from his employer's mine to a nearby dock. He was then employed to provide steam locomotion in substitution for horse power on a short rail line, a task completed in 1825. Meantime the requirements of expanding steam-powered manufacturing had created a substantial volume of freight and passenger business between the large seaport of Liverpool and the interior city of Manchester.

The Liverpool merchants and Manchester manufacturers were not content with the two existing canals and poorly maintained unpaved roads. They were particularly aroused against the canals because from their standpoint the canals seemed to be providing steadily worsening service. They were not dissuaded by the obvious fact that poor service was largely due to the congestion caused by the increasing traffic. In addition they considered the canal toll rates unreasonably high.

The first canal between Liverpool and Manchester was opened about 1725. Within a few years a second one was proposed; the first one fought hard and long against Parliament's approval of this second waterway. A second franchise, when finally granted, resulted in construction of the famous Duke of Bridgewater's canal, completed in 1775. Although at first a symbol of progress, by the 1820's it also seemed to stand in the way of further economic development. In its turn its owners fought against the proposed railroad franchise. Despite canal and agricultural landowner opposition, Parliamentary approval of a railroad was granted in 1825.

In October 1829 this first railroad conducted one of the

world's historic scientific tests. This was a contest between five steam locomotives to determine whether steam power was practicable and, if practicable, whether it also was economic. George Stephenson and his son Robert won the contest with their entry, the Rocket. This was equipped with the world's first usable multitubular-firebox type of steam boiler. The Rocket promptly became the prototype for steam railroad locomotives.

It is almost impossible for modern man to visualize what transportation technology was like when the first steamboats and railroads were being built. Metals were primitive and machine shop processing was crude. Cast iron, wrought iron and brass at that time were assembled into power plants with precision tolerance measured in visible fractions of an inch. Short-lived leather was expected to provide the perfect seal needed between surfaces supposed to be gas-tight, such as between pistons and cylinder walls. Steel was an expensive and scarce material. The hundreds of steel alloys available today were then largely unknown and unavailable. Modern non-ferrous metals and their alloys were little more than laboratory dreams. Rubber, plastics, glass, plywood and even paper were either unknown materials or were primitive in form and usefulness as compared to today.

The steam power plants used by railroad locomotives and paddle wheel steamboats a century ago were not only crude in design and construction; they were unbelievably inefficient in their consumption of fuel. The locomotive went from one cordwood lot to the next one a few miles away; the steamer went relatively short distances from coaling station to coaling station. Its entire hull, including the cargo and passenger spaces, if filled full of coal would not have permitted a really long voyage, such as from England to India. And steam power was the only type of power that had been adapted to transportation. There were no electric motors, no gasoline or diesel motors. Furthermore, the horsepower range was limited; neither very small nor very large steam power units were economic.

By 1860 each of the five present-day modes of transportation was known and had at least experimentally been tried. Of course, the inter-city highways and canals of that time were traversed with the aid of animal rather than steampower. As long-distance carriers they had been made obsolete wherever competing railroads had been constructed, and were being driven out of existence. Thus, the history of mechanized transportation began with proof of a kind of reversed Gresham's Law[1]—that improved transportation drives out older and less desirable existing modes. Some of the regulatory attitudes and actions that likewise have developed during the century since 1860 can be traced in some degree to the emotional resistance generated by so-called railroad ruthlessness toward the picturesque horse-drawn canal boat and the paddle-wheel river steamboat. Today one occasionally hears railroad outcries against similar ruthlessness toward themselves.

Pipelines

The pipeline mode of transportation had become well known and well established by 1860. Water was already being distributed to city homes, offices and factories. Crude oil was first pumped from western Pennsylvania to New York City in 1878. Compressed air was by that time being used to move small parcels and mail through tubes. Of course, today's pipeline shipment of gases, liquids and solids in slurry form represents immense geographical extension and great technical improvement as compared to a century ago. It is interesting that one of the fascinating transportation dreams of inventors was then and is today to find out how to provide self-propulsion and speed control for giant cargo- and person-carrying cars or spheres which would traverse great distances at astonishing speeds and minimum frictional resistance, riding on a cushion of air within a large pipe or rolling in an open semi-circular channel. This intriguing Jules Verne idea of a new kind of pipeline transportation must be left to some great inventive mind of the future.

---

[1] Gresham's famous Law: Bad money drives out good money.

Aviation

The observation balloons used for reconnaisance purposes during the War between the States marked the beginning of aerial evolution. What was for decades little more than a carnival toy has become, as a result of numerous inventions and developments, today's military aircraft and today's commercial aviation. Many of these evolutionary steps in aviation were directly inspired by the government and often were also financed in part or entirely by some interested federal unit.

Highways and canals are rejuvenated

Dramatic indeed was the revival after about 1920 of both commercial highway and canal transportation as important economic modes. In both cases the federal government has played a leading part. It has provided the stimulus of large annual appropriations for federal-aid highways and for canalization of rivers. Private enterprise has been eager to use the new nine-foot canal channels and the newly paved rural highways. They became successful examples of state promotion not only because they were well designed and well built by the government; but even more importantly because they were used by hundreds of private enterprise barge operators and thousands of private enterprise truck and bus operators.

Logistical inter-relations and opportunities recognized

As mechanized transport reduced the world's size, daring businessmen naturally began to dream of creating new trade routes that would actually change economic relations. This bold new concept required private enterprise in transportation to pioneer and the role was soon attempted. An example is the 25-mile Panama Railroad, finished in 1859, that linked up steamship routes between Atlantic ports and Pacific destinations. In 1869 the modern Suez Canal was opened, shortening the all-water route between Europe and India by thousands of miles. Likewise in 1869 the North American continent was spanned by railroad for the first time. It is certain that this use of transportation improvements, to reach still-undeveloped resources or to correct economic unbalance, will be even more important in the future than in the past.

The technological fact of ability to create mass transportation between almost any two points is becoming a major factor in planning to meet urban problems as well as regional and foreign trade needs. The transportation aspects of military operations likewise are being changed. During World War II, for example, the problem of maintenance of the Nationalist China War effort within the heart of Asia was solved by means of the famous Burma Road used by long columns of loaded trucks. After the war Berlin was supplied for an entire winter with coal flown by hundreds of airplanes. Ancient ice islands in the Arctic Ocean have been made temporarily habitable by means of military airlift. In each case adequate mechanized transportation was organized, used and then removed or abandoned. Such military logistics achievements will be commonplace in the future, as will their counterparts of business logistics type.

TODAY'S POSITIVES AND NEGATIVES IN
COMMON CARRIAGE

During the period from about 1860 to about 1940 the familiar logistical elements of present-day common carriage were developed, the railroads being the prototype because of their relatively early and therefore more complete development. There was no pattern to follow. Major problem areas had to be resolved as they presented themselves.

First, the railroads had to work out and adopt physical standardization to the extent necessary to permit interchange of equipment and to meet minimum requirements of the shipper and receiver of freight. Second, the railroads had to develop and adopt sufficiently uniform accounting, billing and tariff publication practices for practicable inter-railroad and customer usage. Third, the government had to develop its concept of regulation and apply it to the users and to the numerous common carrier railroads. These three areas of adequate physical uniformity, sufficient uniformity of paperwork, and uniform and impartial regulation in the public interest have, collectively, created the United States railroad network. The approximately 400 American railroads of today, taken together, have the proud distinction of being the largest and best developed example of the private enterprise type of common carriage in the entire world.

In addition to railroads the other modes also have developed their own distinctive systems of common carriage. Much of their evolution has been by adapting to their own conditions railroad experience as to what to do. These other modes include the American flag subsidized ocean carriers, inland waterway common carrier barge operators, coastwise and Great Lakes vessel operators, petroleum and slurry pipelines, truck and bus common carriers, forwarders and several types of air common carriers. It follows that the United States has become the world leader in number of competitive private enterprises that perform transportation for-hire as common carriers.

Turning now to the transportation situation in the United States as it is today we find that it consists fundamentally of three positives, and three negatives. The first three contribute to the usefulness of transportation to shippers and receivers, and, therefore, to the nation. The other three detract from usefulness, particularly of common carriers. Interacting as they do, these six factors result in what is often called the "Transportation Problem," and thus make business logistics more than an internal management task and skill for users of transportation.

1. *Variety permits adaptation to user need—a plus*

Today there is a wide variety of power, in types as well as size of power plant; there is also a range of available services. Formerly a basic problem was adaptation of freight to the available means of transportation. This was done by limiting size and weight of boxes or bags, and by preventive processing, such as salting of meat, to reduce or avoid damage from the elements. Coordination of the means of transport and the optimum requirements for transportation is a common-place achievement today. Such coordination can, of course, be best attained when new construction or reconstruction from the ground up takes place; it was rarely attained before the steamboat and steam railroad came into existence, and for decades thereafter was not often achieved.

2. *Volume permits efficient utilization of facilities—a plus*

The control of each individual transport unit, such as a vessel or vehicle, is to an ever-increasing extent being accomplished by power-actuated devices that trend toward but have not yet achieved automatic control and performance of steering, acceleration, speed regulation, deceleration and stopping. There is obvious and growing need for such control, including spacing safe distances apart, wherever high traffic volumes must be handled. Efficient movement of concentrated traffic reduces unit cost of transportation. The ultimate in automatic control of highway movement is the radar-guided passenger car, truck or bus; similarly the railroad train can be controlled by means of a prepunched tape or by dispatcher orders transmitted electronically; the modern pipeline already is operated by means of remote-controlled and unmanned pumping stations; the vessel of the future will be kept on course by means of an automatic piloting device; automatic piloting of commercial airplanes and robot guidance of military planes and rockets already are commonplace achievements. Many intermediate steps of innovation and invention must take place before completely automatic operation of any particular high traffic density route can be achieved. Lighter traffic density routes will evolve toward this goal even more slowly.

3. *Normal excess capacity permits stand-by flexibility— a plus*

There is in peacetime a large built-in over-capacity of transportation capability, varying from mode to mode and from time to time. Even though consisting in large part of old, partially worn-out and even obsolete equipment, this over-capacity is vital in meeting the needs caused by recurring peak loads, by high cyclical levels of business activity and also by the dislocations and the peak volume requirements of wartime. The fact that under normal conditions there is a large over-capacity or surplus of transportation capability is well understood by all students of transportation, including Department of Defense planners. Prior to World War II the surplus consisted chiefly in excess capacity of the common carrier railroads. Now there is also some surplus transportation capability inherent in common and contract freight carriers by truck and in the equipment and operating practices of passenger carriers by bus. However, the great reservoir of surplus peacetime transport capacity is in the millions of private passenger automobiles and the hundreds of thousands of private trucks. Viewed as a whole, these automobiles and trucks rarely carry their rated capacity of passengers or freight. Self-propelled vessels and river barges likewise have surplus capacity under normal traffic conditions and this is also true of common carrier and privately operated airplanes.

Since World War II the percentage of inter-city freight carried by railroads has dropped from about 65% to under 50%, although the absolute volume of freight handled by the railroads has remained about the same. In other words the national growth in use of transportation has benefited the other modes. The railroads' curtailment of transportation capability probably has been a factor in causing some users to seek and use other modes to meet their own expanding requirements.

4. *The best transportation is always the least plentiful—*
   a minus

At any given time such as the present moment, there is an inadequate supply of the most desirable transportation facilities and equipment as compared with the potential demand. This is partly because the innovator is necessarily a pioneer whose invention or improvement must first exist in prototype before it can take its proper place, including the ouster of partly worn-out facilities or equipment thus rendered obsolete, and partly to the limitation already noted, that the best coordination of transportation to industrial-user requirements is when both are built new from the ground up. The safest and most efficient railroad transportation is found on high traffic density main-line routes, and these, in general, have been recently rebuilt and modernized. Similarly the best highways and canals are almost always those most recently constructed. The same is true of highway and canal-using equipment, such as trucks and busses, passenger automobiles, barges and tow-boats. Jet aircraft operating over high traffic density routes are another example.

5. *Financial support from private sources is inadequate—a minus*

The inadequate financial support given to common carrier transportation by private enterprise bankers and investors is a present-day symptom reflecting the rise of contract and private carrier competition. It also is due to the indirect pressures exerted by nationalization of transport in foreign countries. No doubt it reflects the trend toward socialism in the United States since the mere knowledge that government is willing to become the source of capital funds acts as a deterrent against private investment. Prior to World War I, nearly all new investment in inter-city and intra-city transportation in the United States came from private sources. Steam and electric railroads of that time provided their own rights-of-way, their own tracks and stations, and their own rolling stock. Great Lakes and coastwise steamship operations were likewise privately owned, as were in most cases their port facilities. There were also privately owned pipelines, and this mode remains today flourishing and privately financed. Since 1917, aside from pipelines, government has gradually emerged as the major source of capital for construction of new or improved transportation routes. Examples are roads, canals, and airports. To a lesser but growing extent, government is also becoming an owner of transportation equipment and a guarantor of equipment loans. It is probable that government today supplies a major part of the annual capital investment made in transportation in the United States, other than for purchase of owner-driven trucks and automobiles. The result has been growing reluctance of bankers and other private investors to provide capital funds by buying newly issued transportation securities. This, of course, has been most apparent with respect to common stock rather than bonds or mortgages, and most serious with respect to railroad financing.

6. *Regulation hinders competition with unregulated carriage—a minus*

Common carriers generally complain of an inadequate degree of freedom within the boundaries created by regulation. In other words each common carrier mode has its own details of criticism of today's regulatory laws, procedures and decisions. Having developed in the past, regulation may not yet adequately reflect today's competitive conditions between carriers and modes. This is especially true of the *entry upon and abandonment of service* controls inherited from the past; and of the quarrel-generating competitive zones between the modes and between common carriage and contract, exempt, and private carriage. With five modes of transportation, each consisting of numerous separate private enterprises, there can be no doubt that competitive facts and pressures are dominant. Competition of all common carriers is not only with each other; even more importantly it is with contract, exempt and private carriage.

It follows that within the established five modes of common carriage, there is ample evidence of the effects of strong intramodal and intermodal competitive factors. The degree and extent of government regulation is greatest over common carriers, is less over contract carriers, and still less over the special kind of contract-type carriers that handle exempt commodities. Of course regulation of private carriage is very slight, being limited to safety matters and to prevention of some actions that constitute carriage-for-hire. Thus the effects of over-regulation and antiquated regulation are chiefly the burden of railroad and other common carriers, for whom the regulation was primarily designed.

TRANSPORTATION IN 1999

In 1999, there will be nine kinds of transportation to which, for convenience, we can apply the term "modes." There will be railroads, carriers by highway, carriers by pipeline, users of the ocean and of inland and coastwise navigation channels, air carriers including hovercraft, and carriers by cableway or belt conveyor, all modernized and greatly improved as the result of technical developments. There will also be carriers which own and operate interchangeable equipment, such as the already familiar detachable truck bodies. In addition to these seven kinds of carriage-for-hire, there will be government transportation activities, and there will be the constantly growing use of private transportation, both so distinctive in their economic impact as to justify classification as modes. That 1999 will not be like the present seems certain, even though no new transportation device comparable in effect to the automobile of 1905 or the airplane of 1925 can now be foreseen.

Rationalization of rail-highway freight carriage

Prior to the World War I period of federal control and operation, railroad freight lines and services were in balance and were not in need of rationalization. On the contrary, up to about 1920, they were well adapted to the needs of the nation. Since then they have become gradually more maladjusted and more obsolete when viewed as a national network and not as individual railroads.

Three major factors have created this unbalance. First, there has been a relative shift of population and industry away from the northeastern states. Second is the impact of competitive modes of transportation throughout the nation. Third, difficult financial problems of adjusting particular railroads built for both passenger and freight service to the decline or disappearance of passenger trains have developed. Fourth, the flexibility of railroad's major competitor, the truck, because it is not tied to fixed locations or routes has attracted users even at somewhat higher charges.

In the northeast, the railroad system has become relatively

too extensive because of these trends. Fortunately in the south and west, the problem of relative size of railroad plant in relation to demand is less acute.

To rearrange and improve the common carrier railroads, that is to rationalize them so that they will continue to be a major mode of transportation, requires planning for future needs, followed by accomplishment. By 1999 both these steps in the rationalization process will have been accomplished.

The immediate problem is to get the planning phase started as a voluntary rather than a government effort. Underlying the planning there must be research. It is encouraging that a start in this direction has been made in one of the important areas that must be rationalized, namely, freight rates. Research committees with competent personnel are now attached to the major ratemaking bureaus. This is a bold change since some of these committees have operated without benefit of thorough and careful research for seventy or more years. The main research objective is to find out what kinds of freight rates attract and retain desirable traffic. The current interest on the part of railroads in contract-type freight rates, such as the so-called "agreed rates" used in Europe and Canada is an example of this new research viewpoint.

Rationalization is not an untried fad idea. It is a technique that has been used in other countries, for example, in Great Britain after the First World War. It is necessary because it provides a broad approach to those basic railroad problems that are themselves nation-wide in character. Solution of national problems requires a national approach. If voluntary rationalization is not accomplished, then compulsory nationalization of American railroads may become inevitable. Nationalization in other countries has been the costly socialistic way to attempt nation-wide solution of basic railroad problems. Nationalization has solved few problems, but wherever carried out it has destroyed common carrier railroads as private enterprises.

By 1999 highway congestion will have forced the rail-truck partnership called "piggy-back" or "trailer-on-flatcar" to develop to its economic optimum. Common and contract truckers will then offer, at distances over about 300 miles, the advantages of exact origin to actual destination movements, but will load their trailers or truck bodies on rail flatcars for part or all of the distance, performing by highway only the metropolitan area trips over city streets at each end. This use of "piggyback" will result in gradual decline in intensity of competition between rail and truck, as each finds its own best economic sphere, and as each learns how to use the inherent advantages of the other mode of transportation in its own behalf. In itself, this will be a major rationalization accomplishment.

Rationalization of freight carriage on inland waterways

In 1999 the domestic water carriers by barge and vessel will have developed and made their own present degree of rationalization even more effective. They will continue to be well adjusted to their potential market. There will be even greater and more efficient use of navigation channels, and hopefully less political "hue and cry." The question of "user charges" by 1999 may have lost its political overtones and have been settled. Settlement, even if it means partial or complete reimbursement of federal expenditures on behalf of navigation, probably will not lessen or greatly retard the growth of freight transportation by barge or vessel in competition with railroads and highways. The enormous growth of the United States population-wise and in economic ways will continue to provide steadily increasing need for water transportation.

Pipelines have developed rationally

Since about 1880, pipelines, the fourth mode, have become an interconnected network resembling the national railroad system. In addition to water and crude oil, pipelines carry refined petroleum products, natural gas, and "slurry," that is, certain finely powdered solid materials such as coal suspended in a suitable liquid. Pipelines will continue to be the only mode of transport that moves in only one direction. There is no costly return movement of empty or partly loaded equipment to deal with. There is no rationalization problem, either now or in the future.

Pipelines have been built only to meet known demands. When the demand disappears, they go out of use. When improvements, such as larger diameter pipe, become available, the obsolete pipelines are not forced to remain unchanged as a result of regulatory or court procedures that contrive to bring about indefinite delays. Government agencies do not provide "promotional" funds for acquisition of rights-of-way, construction of terminal storage tanks or creation of new subsidized pipelines. Because of its unique characteristics, the pipeline mode of transport in 1999 will still be following its rational private enterprise policies and actions.

Rationalization of air carriers

The fifth major mode of transportation is commercial air navigation. Its development dates from about 1930. Its technical evolution has been extremely rapid, yet further great changes are in sight. The use of jet power and the development of commercial helicopters and of airplanes that require only a small landing strip are opening new commercial possibilities for both freight and passenger service. Both for defense and national development reasons there has been a bountiful flow of government "promotional" funds into airplane design, airway lighting and control, and airport construction and operation.

These promotional activities, coupled with the concurrent evolution of domestic and international civil air law and regulation, all have combined to produce and maintain an irrational and unbalanced pattern.

The railroad mode of transport, as pointed out, is no longer rationally in economic balance with national needs. This is because it has been to some extent prevented from adjusting itself during the years since the rise of rival competing modes of transport. Commercial aviation in the United States has not yet achieved economic balance. The basic concept of government has been to promote, that is, to hasten commercial air development in advance of proven need. Thus, but for quite a different reason, commercial aviation is as much in need of rationalization as are the railroads. And like the railroad problem the failure to rationalize can lead to nationalization by the federal government, already a major partner through its past and present promotional expenditures. Like the railroads, commercial aviation can and should fear nationalization, already the aviation pattern in most of the nations of the world.

In 1999, less than forty years from now, the commercial aviation common and contract carriers will have accomplished voluntary rationalization, and thus averted the undesirable socialistic alternative, nationalization. Aviation will have come of age. It will have made further competitive gains at the expense of other forms of transportation, particularly in the field of passenger transport.

Rationalization of cableways and belt conveyors

Although by no means as yet of major importance, the sixth mode of transportation, the growing use of cableways and belt conveyors, should not be overlooked. The ski tow and other mountain or canyon cableways have opened up otherwise inaccessible areas for passenger travel or for mining operations. The belt conveyor and its passenger counterpart, the moving stairway or platform, already perform gigantic daily tasks of moving materials or persons. To date both cableways and conveyors are relatively short-haul transportation devices, but this is an economic rather than a technical limitation. Because local in present-day application, there is as yet no federal regulation. Outside of some defense interest, there has been no federal promotional activity. Hence these devices are making their way solely for rational economic reasons. In 1999, this rational development will have continued, largely as desirable supplementation but also to some extent as a competitive mode of transport.

Forwarders will make rational use of inter-modal possibilities

The distinguishing feature of the forwarder, himself a common carrier, is in his use of common or contract carriage supplied by others in any combination and to whatever extent desired. Variations of the forwarder, viewed as a technique for handling packages and small shipments, include express companies and parcel post. Forwarders have recently begun to use improved containers that are interchangeable between different modes of transportation. These containers vary in size up to 40-foot van-type truck bodies. Two truck bodies or two complete truck trailers can be carried on an 85-foot flatcar. They can also be loaded quickly into a barge or vessel. For example, merchandise loaded in a factory that does not have a rail siding can be trucked in its locked container to a railroad yard, moved by rail, then by barge, then by vessel, to a destination in our 49th or 50th state. In Alaska or Hawaii or Puerto Rico the container and contents can be moved by truck or rail or air to destination. In the entire journey there has been no transfer of lading. The original container door seals will still be intact at the customer's door.

This new kind of "forwarding" is truly a seventh mode of transport since it uses the other modes as required and thus furnishes new through routes and services not otherwise available without costly and damaging transfer. From the standpoint of the shipper and receiver the container becomes the vehicle for transportation. By 1999 forwarder transportation using various types of containers will be available from anywhere to anywhere. This new mode of transportation will develop because it fills an economic need. To the extent that it does, it obviously is rationalized, that it, it is and will continue to be in economic balance with its market.

Government operation will become a distinctive transportation area

By 1999 government-furnished transportation will be recognized as an eighth and distinct mode of transport. Today the growing pains involved in emergence of government direct participation in operation of transportation-for-hire are apparent. The vital question that will be answered during the next forty years is how much farther this participation will extend.

The direct participation is, of course, in addition to government promotional activities such as provision of highways, airways, and navigation channels.

Government already is operating busses and subway trains, and also is providing financial assistance to some railroad commuter services. The school bus is becoming universal, not only in rural but also in metropolitan areas. The municipal airport is a transportation device similar to the privately owned rail or bus terminal. Another local area activity is federal operation of a large fleet of trucks to handle mail and parcel post.

The federal government operates Alaska's only railroad. Throughout the world extend the routes of the Military Air Transportation Service and the Military Sea Transportation Service. Passenger automobiles, busses and trucks are supplied for military use in and near military bases. Canals, navigable river or lake or harbor channels, locks and lighthouses all are transportation.

One distinctive characteristic of government transportation, both in local areas and of defense type, is that the user is not expected to pay the full cost. The general taxpayer makes up the difference or *foots the entire bill.* Herein lies possible unfairness. If a government-operated subway system gives a 25¢ ride for 15¢, the private enterprise bus line or railroad offering commuter service in the same area may not be able to charge an adequate fare for its services. Similarly if a military airplane or steamship takes all of the most desirable cargo the private enterprise steamship or air operator may find his operation unprofitable for lack of sufficient traffic revenue.

Private carriage also needs rationalization

The ninth mode is private transportation. Like forwarder and government transport, this mode is not identified as a technically distinctive kind of transportation, since it uses all kinds as required. The private automobile now dominates passenger transportation and will continue to do so. The private truck now dominates local freight transportation and it will continue to do so. Hence the importance of private transport cannot be exaggerated.

By 1999 the use of private means of transport will be greater than ever. Whenever sufficient volume of freight exists a private railroad or truck operation, or pipeline, or barge or vessel operation may have become appropriate. Many such private transportation activities will have come into existence. This is another way of saying that private transportation of freight will be competing wherever possible with common or contract carriers. From the standpoint of the established carrier for hire, private transportation will continue to skim the cream, that is, the most desirable freight.

However, rationalization must become the rule in this area also. We know that increasing population will result in congestion of available highways, railroads, waterways and airways. Additional routes are becoming more difficult to create. Hence the great future opportunity for expansion of private transportation is not in built-up communities but in sparsely settled areas.

Already it is obvious that private transportation must do much of the economic pioneering in undeveloped or underdeveloped areas, for example, in Alaska. It follows that, though potentially competitive with all the established modes of transportation, private carriage of freight over long distances should tend more to supplement than to compete with other modes.

Proliferation of the modes or distinctive kinds of transportation is itself of logistical importance. The more modes, including the variations within each mode, the greater the flexibility and usefulness of transportation to the nation and to industry and commerce. Business logistics decisions can thus be more perfectly adapted to the requirements of the particular enterprise. And the transportation element can be either emphasized or subordinated, in order to arrive at its optimum combination with the other logistical elements such as purchasing, production scheduling, inventory control, and warehouse location.

SUMMARY

This chapter has discussed transportation, its modal pro-liferation, its common carrier problem, and its growing need for rationalization. Transportation serves the entire public. Therefore, it includes more than business logistics since the lat-ter is limited to transportation that is used and useful in busi-ness transactions. In its turn business logistics includes more than transportation.

Business logistics encompasses every aspect of *place* and *time* utilities that are created to facilitate production and sale of goods or services by an enterprise. Transportation is com-monly limited to mean only movements accomplished by me-chanical devices suitable for use by common carriers (whether actually used by common carriers, or by contract carriers, in private carriage or by government for its own shipments). For example, use of fork-lift carriers, "straddle-lift" carriers, or belt conveyors to move finished products from inventory to a trailer or freight car is not considered to be transportation even through such movement to the "loading point" is clearly indis-pensable in creating the desired *place* and *time* utilities.

Business logistics includes both *planning* and *physical han-dling* activities.

Planning activities include:

1. Selecting devices and scheduling their use in handling raw materials both before and after transportation.
2. Determining and managing raw material inventory levels, whether purchased or produced.
3. Coordinating and scheduling production "runs" to meet sales requirements, to avoid month-end production crises and to maintain finished product inventories at optimum levels.
4. Selecting and scheduling transportation and warehous-ing requirements, and developing effective "paperwork" procedures.

Physical handling activities include:

5. Raw material in-plan movements, also stocking and de-

stocking, also loading into and unloading from transportation devices.

6. Work-in-process storage and delivery at work places where and when needed, to the extent that such movements cannot appropriately be performed as an aspect of production.

7. Finished product packaging or palletizing for shipment, warehousing at or near point of production, loading into transportation devices and shipment to a customer or to a break-bulk type of branch warehouse.

8. Unloading and warehousing at break-bulk point, processing (if required) and rearranging, reloading and final shipment.

The relative importance of transportation has been increasing from the standpoint of business logistics. The increase in use of private carriage, either for the entire journey or as supplement at one or both ends of a for-hire journey has lengthened the mechanized portion definable as transportation. The cost of inter-modal transfers has been reduced, and the "service" has been improved by mechanization of such transfers. Thus carriers have gained "know-how" useful to business logistics in tackling its own similar problems at either end of the transportation. Most important, carriers and business logistics executives have begun to think of transportation as one of the parts of the total journey. Thus the concept sometimes called *total transportation* is becoming dominant, a concept that requires cooperative planning and effective joint actions.

By 1999, American transportation will be more rational in pattern and performance. It will be well adjusted to the needs of a very much larger nation, populationwise and industrywise, than at present. But achievement of this goal will not occur without, as Winston Churchill used to tell the British people during World War II, "blood, sweat and tears."

Chapter III

THE USER VIEW OF TRANSPORTATION AS ONE SYSTEM

When an individual decides to go from A to B, his interest is in using transportation to make his journey faster, easier, less expensive, or more comfortable and convenient, according to his own evaluation of these factors. He does not separate possible use of a private automobile or a chartered bus, or a common carrier railroad or airline in either a modal or a legal sense. He thinks of all of them as different ways of going from A to B. He chooses the method best suited from his point of view.

Similarly industrial and commercial users of freight transportation are not loyal to any mode or combination of modes. Often users have no loyalty to particular freight carriers. Users think of modern mechanized devices for moving freight from A to B as "transportation." Hence, the concept of all transportation as being one national system is in accord with their logistics thinking.

Furthermore, users think of transportation as consisting of all the sequential movements that result in a personal journey or a freight movement from actual origin to final destination. Transportation is not just the segment called a railroad or a truck line.

Both personal travel and freight movements have acquired new and greater mobility as the result of development of private transport and of multi-modal competition of carriers. Mobility is a concept that goes beyond mere freedom of choice. It includes ability to change from one's original choice to another, even in the midst of a journey. It includes ability to suit one's own convenience as to time of departure or of arrival at destina-

45

tion. For the individual the private automobile has provided greater personal freedom in such important matters as location of home and work place, choice of friends, and choice of leisure activities. These mobility gains are precious, and would not be readily given up. Neither the millions of private owner-operators nor the corporations engaged in performing private carriage for themselves, as well as the monopolistic nationalized transportation agencies, would willingly accept external co-ordination or control no matter how it is organized. On the one hand, the numerous private operators of their own transportation devices do not desire to be organized or regimented. On the other, the nationalized agencies tend to consider their own organization and policies adequate.

It is important to remember an obvious but often overlooked fact that although users can and do regard transportation as one system, there is no such thing as a single transportation industry. Instead there are millions of individuals and thousands of corporations performing transportation, some solely for themselves and some operating on a for-hire basis. Improvement in transportation industry organization is a broad subject that cannot be limited to one aspect such as the plight of the private enterprise railroads or the future of state-financed toll highways.

GREATER MECHANIZATION OF TRANSPORTATION IS NEEDED

Congestion is becoming a major transportation problem. It is due to population growth, and up to now has been only partially offset by the efficiency gains derived from concentrating and controlling traffic, for example, on four-lane highways. Congestion is caused not only by the volume of traffic in relation to route capacity but also by the presence of "choke points." Hence route capacity depends upon physical characteristics, upon effective control of traffic flow, and upon discovery and elimination of choke points as they develop.

On a railroad this means roadbed and track of adequate

strength, ruling grade and curvature; proper signalling such as centralized traffic control (CTC); and elimination of situations such as grade crossings, or passage along city streets requiring "slow orders." On a highway this means roadway of adequate strength, ruling grade and curvature; proper signalling or, preferably, elimination of the need for signal control; and elimination of choke points by grade separation and by providing extra lanes for slow traffic. For air carriers a serious choke point exists at airports, particularly when weather conditions cause incoming planes to be "stacked" waiting for permission to land.

Congestion creates large volumes of concentrated traffic. Volume justifies the capital cost of mechanized guidance systems as well as route improvement. The commercial airplane's automatic piloting device and the even more complete devices for directing crewless robot airplanes from a ground control station are examples of this trend. Such devices change the nature of human participation from machine operator to machine maintainers and observers.

In summary, there are three kinds of human participation in transportation, as manual laborer, as machine operator, and as machine maintainer. The trend is toward as little manual labor as possible and toward the use of mechanized guidance systems where volume warrants. Clearly the goal is attainment of the practicable maximum of mechanization. Such a goal has important effects upon transportation industry organization, especially of common carriers.

Common carrier mergers facilitate mechanization

Within the common carrier group there have been many proofs of the economies of concentration of volume. Past experience points to merger as leading toward improved organization, in part because with greater volume its executives will be able to make more rational decisions. Mergers that cut across one or more modes may likewise be able to achieve economies of scale. However such "department store type" mergers are more difficult to achieve, because they are more likely to run afoul of the regulatory prohibition against "unduly lessening competition." The important point from the standpoint of improved organization is that some mergers can and do result in more efficient carriers. This organization improvement stems in large part from the ability to so schedule larger volumes of traffic as to concentrate it more effectively.

Rearrangement of routings and schedules usually results in reduction of circuity as well as in concentration of larger volumes of traffic upon the selected high-density routes. In the case of a railroad merger some track formerly needed may be abandoned. Some may be downgraded from mainline to branchline. The remaining tracks will then have traffic volume sufficient to justify the cost of installation of automatic control devices. In the case of trucker mergers, important savings of route-mileage also can result. In addition rearrangement of truck schedules and relocation of transfer terminals can increase the effective utilization of equipment.

Increased mechanization of paperwork also is necessary

Common carriers spend a large part of their income and effort upon construction, operation and maintenance of equipment on the one hand and their immense mountains of paperwork on the other hand. The clerical aspects of moving billions of shipments ranging from small parcels to train loads and ship loads is stupendous. In and of itself paperwork is an obstacle that discourages use of common carriers and encourages use of contract and private carriage.

Within each common carrier enterprise, if it is large enough, use of modern electronic memory storage and high-speed data-processing office machinery is an important step forward. Here again merger of the smaller common carriers into larger units improves transportation industry organization by making possible these economies of scale.

Viewing the transportation of goods by common carriers as a whole we see that mechanization of paperwork within each company is only part of the problem. The complex procedures required for collection and division of freight revenue between several carriers who join together in forming a through route is an example. In Great Britain these transactions between railroad common carriers began to be handled by a central clearing house more than a century ago. Establishment of similar central clearing houses for use by air, truck, and rail common carriers is still in its infancy or experimental stage in the United States. The need is evident and the improvement in organization and in efficiency is obvious.

An even more difficult and important problem is the transfer of freight rate information from paperbound printed tariffs to the new type of memory storage- and data-processing machinery. This is a huge task involving several trillion individual freight rates now printed in thousands of state and interstate tariffs. There is as yet no common coding possible since even the simplest articles are classified in different manner by different rail, truck, or other classification committees. Freight tariff simplification, likewise essential to mechanization of this paperwork task, has made little progress despite strenuous efforts by the government and by industry groups. Because this task is so large and affects so many interests, it will take many years to accomplish. Nevertheless improved organization and effectiveness of the common carrier segment of transportation in the United States requires ultimate achievement and success.

Common carrier trends point toward the one system-concept

Three common carrier problems have been reviewed: coping with increasing congestion; achieving greater efficiency by concentrating traffic in various ways including mergers; and reducing and rationalizing the paperwork burden. Viewed together, these point to greater dependence of carriers upon each other. They must, collectively, cooperate to reduce congestion and at the same time concentrate traffic in more efficient ways. They must enter into joint study and operating arrangements that will lead to better handling of paperwork. Thus the one-system concept is developing among carriers, as well as in user thinking.

UNREGULATED VS. REGULATED TRANSPORTATION

The impact of legal status upon organization is important. Its organizational effects are the result of economic and political rather than safety or efficiency considerations. From the economic and political standpoint there are unregulated, regulated and nationalized kinds of transportation.

Most unregulated transportation is private, that is, has been undertaken by the owner of the freight being transported or by the driver of one's own automobile. However, some "for-hire" transportation in the United States, such as the carriage of agricultural products, has been exempted from economic regulation. Both categories, exempt and private, have been growing steadily. Unregulated transportation offers convenience as well as adaptability to actual transport needs. Unregulated transporters-for-hire often can operate at lower unit cost and, therefore, make lower charges than can a regulated carrier. This is especially the case where there is volume movement in one direction and some return haul in the other. In addition private and exempt carriers do not impose complex and costly paperwork problems on their users, as common carriers must do.

Private enterprise is not disappearing in transportation

Private enterprise in for-hire carrier transportation is not disappearing. However it is being replaced in certain portions of the transportation field by a combination of private operation supplemented by government ownership and operation. An example is the private automobile and the highway. Government supplementation also consists in provision and maintenance of air and water navigation facilities that are used for private carriage, and by the government for its nationalized transportation activities.

Private enterprise in transportation is flourishing in the unregulated area. On the other hand private enterprise is fading in the common carrier type of activity, particularly railroads. In most countries outside the United States the major type of common carrier, the railroad, already has been nationalized. In the United States the common carrier railroads are, with the exception of the Alaska Railroad, still private enterprises; but viewed as a whole they can scarcely be said to be flourishing. Government-owned commuter transportation is gradually taking the place of its predecessors—regulated common carriers.

ORGANIZATIONAL CHANGES ARE TAKING PLACE

Transportation within the United States is more adequate than anywhere else in the world. There is here more variety and also more competitive duplication, both between modes and within modes. With the different stages of development of the five major modes, and the different situations of individual carrier companies, it is obvious that opportunities for improvements in over-all organization are bound to be present.

A very basic principle of organization is to separate as much as possible those activities that should compete with each other. Common carriers are a good example since there is and should be vigorous inter-carrier competition despite as well as because of regulatory rules and procedures. Railroads should and do compete aggressively with other railroads and also with truck carriers, barge carriers, and with private carriage. Indeed government's relation to regulated carriers often is that of umpire. Government first determines the rules of fair competition and then has to enforce them through its regulatory decisions.

Development of the five modes of mechanized transportatation has not only increased the cost and the average size of carrier equipment; it also has established ever-higher standards for the routes to be used. Thus river channels must be made deeper and wider. Roads must be stronger, wider, smoother and must be designed with adequate grade separation or traffic control signal lights. Airlanes and airports inevitably become more and more complex and costly as air congestion grows.

For nearly half a century beginning about 1860, the Federal Government encouraged railroad building by land-grant and other aids. Since about 1910, it has spent billions of dollars for construction and for subsequent maintenance of improved, and then improved again, water, highway and air routes. Railroads and pipelines on the other hand have continued to develop and improve their privately owned and maintained routes. They too have spent vast sums of money for these purposes.

In recent years railroads have raised a question as to the role of government in improving river, highway and air routes. They claim that government is not applying to its own conduct the organization maxim as to the desirability of separation of activities that should compete. In effect, they argue that government builds better routes for the other three modes and at the same time regulates the railroads in such a way as to retard or even to prevent them from competing effectively with the barges, trucks and airplanes that are using the government-provided routes.

There can be little doubt that the Federal Government in the past did encourage the creation and development of barge, truck and air common carriers. It wanted them as users of its expensive river, highway and air routes. Likewise government heeded and agreed with the argument that it should use government funds to create competition of "yardstick" type for the established railroad common carriers.

The high point of government encouragement of intermodal competition was about 1925. Since then a more friendly attitude toward established common carriers seems to be developing. The Department of Commerce reports to Congress of recent years and President Kennedy's Message to Congress in April, 1962, all favor somewhat less restrictive regulation of railroads and other common carriers as a means for equalizing competition.

The controversy between America's private enterprise common carrier railroads and the various government agencies that today are spending public funds to improve and maintain river channels, highways, and air routes brings out the important fact that industry and government affect each other. It is clear that railroads will survive as private enterprises only if they are not so restricted by government as to be unable to continue to improve their own privately owned tracks and related structures.

Common carriers are now a small part
of the transportation system

Planning, financing, locating, constructing and maintaining mile after mile of water, highway, air, railroad or pipeline routes are as much parts of the over-all transportation system as is the equipment used thereon. The distinction between creation of a route and its use has been growing in importance because of the dominance of government activity in the former and of private activity in the latter. Although an ominously growing factor, there is today only a tiny fraction of equipment ownership and operation in the hands of some designated government agency. All the rest is privately owned and operated.

Many of the nation's common carriers bear names that are universally known and respected. However, common carriers are, despite their importance, in a minority position when compared to the millions of private automobiles and trucks and the hundreds of privately owned and operated barges and airplanes, as well as the contract type of carrier. Only the pipeline and rail common carriers are dominant within their own mode of transport.

The Transportation Association of America annually measures the gradual loss of position of the common carriers. Its estimate for 1961 was that, out of about 53 billions of dollars spent for *passenger transportation*, 87 per cent went for purchase, maintenance and operation of private automobiles and nearly 2 per cent for private aircraft. The remaining 11 per cent, or about 6 billion dollars, was the share of common carriers. The railroads earned about 700 million dollars by carrying inter-city and commuter passengers. This was 1.3 per cent of the total and about one-ninth of the portion going to all the common carriers for carriage of passengers.

Its estimate of 1961 *freight transportation*, exclusive of international movements, was that it cost American users about

43 billions of dollars. Less than $10 billions, or about 23 per cent of this amount, was spent for rail transportation, including costs assumed by the user in loading and unloading freight cars and also assuming that most of the express and forwarder transportation was by rail. This compares with the estimated $19 billions, or about 44 per cent, received as freight revenue by inter-city trucks, both fully and partially regulated.

These freight data also show that the common carriers fully regulated by the Interstate Commerce Commission or the Civil Aeronautics Board (rail, truck, barge, coastwise, pipeline, express, forwarder and air, other than international) received in 1961 about $19 billions or about 44 per cent of the total freight costs paid by users. Within this $19 billions spent for fully regulated freight service, inter-city trucks received 38 per cent and railroad gross revenue accounted for 43 per cent. The remainder, or $24 billions, came to 56 per cent of the total freight transportation cost of $43 billions. This was paid by users for private, exempt or other non-common carrier freight transportation. These Transportation Association of America estimates total 96 billions of dollars for freight and passenger transportation combined. This means that about one-sixth of annual Gross National Product was derived from creation of *place* and *time* utilities in 1961; of this 26 per cent was the share obtained by all modes of common carriage.

THE TRANSPORTATION PROBLEM IN 1933 AND 1961

An association executive is pictured in a recent publication surrounded by the bound volumes of studies of transportation problems made in recent years by the government or by associations, foundations and individuals. He is pleading for more remedial action and fewer words. During the years since 1807, when the first study of this kind was sent to the President and Congress by Albert Gallatin, there have been hundreds of such reports prepared, printed and shelved.

An interesting and instructive exercise is to pick at random one of these studies and compare it with today. From such a comparison some measure of our progress toward solution of problems may become possible. The study selected from the past is Dr. G. Lloyd Wilson's book on The Transportation Crisis of 1933. This out-of-print book contains 327 pages of scholarly analysis and forceful recommendations.

Before quoting from Doctor Wilson's book, we should recall the setting. The United States in the short space of about 15 years, from 1917 to 1933, had participated in World War I; had experimented for more than two years beginning in late 1917 with nationalization of railroads and other carriers; and had gone through the readjustment years of the 1920's often referred to as the "profitless prosperity" years. The boom that developed in the late 1920's had culminated in the stock market crash in 1929. Although no one in 1933 felt quite sure that the greatest depression of our history had at last reached its bottom we can look back to see that this was in fact happening. In 1933 there were ample reasons to describe current national transportation problems as of crisis character. It is startling that Lloyd Wilson's words, written as they were in an atmosphere of general gloom and depression, seem quite appropriate today. The following paragraphs present the substance of this book in his own words. They will seem amazingly applicable to transportation problems of today.

Dr. Wilson's views in 1933

"Transportation in the United States is in a state of chaos. Business depression, political uncertainty, financial stringency, destructive competition, vacillating policy, and public apathy have conspired to shake to the foundations one of the strongest American institutions, the transportation system.[1]

"The deplorable and alarming condition of affairs affecting all carriers in the field of transportation can be traced to several well-defined causes. First, the economic depression. . . . Second, intense competition, of an unwise nature due principally to the establishment of transportation facilities

[1] The Transportation Crisis, G. Lloyd Wilson, Sears Publishing Co., New York, New York, 1933, preface vii.

of various kinds in excess of the number actually needed.
. . . Third, the inconsistent policies of governmental regulation. . . . Fourth, the participation of the Federal Government in the transportation business in competition with
privately owned and operated [carriers-for-hire]. . . .
Fifth, the failure to coordinate existing transportation facilities into an integrated national system.[2]

"At the present time there is unquestionably a surplus of
transportation facilities far in excess of the facilities required. The transportation problem of the present is not
to increase or extend the [common carrier] transportation
system, but to salvage the existing facilities by coordinating
and developing each type of [common] carrier in the interests of all carriers and of the public.[3]

"The present railroad regulation policy was framed and
has been developed . . . upon the assumption that the railroads enjoyed a substantial monopoly of domestic transportation. . . . The time has come to adopt a broad comprehensive policy of regulation of the whole transportation
industry . . . in which each type of carrier has its proper
place determined by its relative efficiency.[4]

"The regulatory policies and practices of the several state
governments should be harmonized and reconciled with one
another and with Federal regulatory policies and practices. . . .[5]

"In conclusion it is suggested that all forms of interstate
transportation for hire . . . be regulated by one governmental agency . . . with respect to standards of service,
rates and fares, publication of tariffs, finances and securities, accounts and statistics, intercarrier relations and arrangements, public relations and employee relations."[6]

Railroad common carriers in 1933

Dr. Wilson's book emphasized the plight of the railroads,
as shown in the following quotations:

---

[2] *Ibid.*, p. 2.
[3] *Ibid.*, p. 30.
[4] *Ibid.*, p. 300.
[5] *Ibid.*, p. 326.
[6] *Ibid.*, p. 325.

"The railroads are suffering from depleted revenues, reduced freight tonnage, and decreased passenger traffic. . . .[7]

"Many of the railroad stations and other terminal facilities are competitive duplications of the corresponding facilities of other carriers which can be used to capacity only in periods of peak traffic.[8]

"The size of railroad organization . . . the complicated rate structures, the detailed and often burdensome requirements governing packing, . . . the rigidity of railroad rates and charges all contribute to the diversion of freight from the rails to the highways.[9]

"Among the steps apparently necessary . . . are . . . simplification . . . of . . . classification . . . [and] freight rate structures; the publication of tariffs in more simple and understandable form . . . [and] lower rates than carload rates upon movements of a number of carload shipments at one time from one point of origin to one destination.[10]

"All railroads [should be consolidated] in a limited number of large systems, preferably in a plan of consolidation to be agreed upon by the railroads and their owners, which will reduce inter-railroad competition to the greatest degree possible . . . no detailed preconceived plan should be forced upon the railroads in this period of crisis."[11]

Highway transportation in 1933

Professor Wilson saw clearly that common and contract carriers by truck were a new and very important form or mode of transportation even though, in 1933, it was just beginning. His statements are as follows:

"Motor truck carriers are feeling the inevitable effects of destructive competition due to the vast number of common carriers, contract carriers, and private trucks and busses,

----

[7] *Ibid.*, p. 1.
[8] *Ibid.*, p. 17.
[9] *Ibid.*, pp. 284–85.
[10] *Ibid.*, pp. 285–86.
[11] *Ibid.*, p. 320.

as well as the bitter competition between motor carriers and other means of transportation.[12]

"The private automobile has been the greatest destroyer of railroad passenger traffic, while the privately owned and operated freight truck has diverted large quantities of freight traffic from the railroads [and] steamship lines. . . ."[13]

"The motor transportation business is an established fact in American transportation. It cannot and should not be reduced in scope or influence. The railroads [and] steamship lines . . . must adapt their services to conditions [by establishing] . . . door-to-door freight services at rates not higher than competitive motor truck rates . . . [by increasing] the speed of service . . . [and by simplification of] the freight classification rules and regulations . . . [and] packing requirements.[14]

"The coordination of motor and rail transportation may be effected through the ownership and operation of automotive vehicles by the railroad companies . . . by the establishment of agency arrangements . . . or by the establishment of joint services and through routes and rates by railroad and motor transportation companies."[15]

Waterway and air transportation in 1933

Lloyd Wilson knew that the new common carriers by barge on inland waterways and by air over government-established airways also were to become important modes of transportation. He discussed them as follows:

"One of the most controversial problems in transportation is the inland waterways question. Millions of dollars of Federal funds have been spent on inland waterways, principally to make them navigable. . . ."[16]

"The coordination of rail and water transportation in the coastwise, intercoastal, Great Lakes and inland waterway

---

[12] *Ibid.*, p. 1.
[13] *Ibid.*, p. 21.
[14] *Ibid.*, p. 180.
[15] *Ibid.*, p. 324.
[16] *Ibid.*, p. 9.

services through common ownership, management or control [is suggested].[17]
"Despite adverse business conditions, the air transport industry continues to grow in facilities and traffic.[18]
"This rapidly growing air transport industry is operating over Federal . . . airways, between municipally . . . owned airports."[19]

For contrast with today, choice has been made of the 1961 Federal report on National Transportation Policy, designated as a Committee Print, 87th Congress, First Session and called the Preliminary Draft of a Report prepared for the Committee on Interstate and Foreign Commerce, United States Senate, by a Special Study Group. This study has been christened the "Doyle Report" after its staff director, retired Air Force Major General John P. Doyle. It boasts 730 carefully written pages in rather small type, so that it contains at least three times as many words as in the 1933 book by G. Lloyd Wilson.

Wilson and Doyle views compared

It will be recalled that Lloyd Wilson said that "Business depression, political uncertainty, financial stringency, destructive competition, vacillating policy, and public apathy have conspired to shake to the foundations one of the strongest American institutions, the transportation system." Of course, in 1933 he was referring to the common carriers and particularly to the railroads as "the transportation system." Present-day usage applies the term, transportation system, to all transportation facilities, of every kind and mode.

In a section of the Doyle Report headed by the subtitle, Conclusions, we read the following:

"Technology, uncoordinated and expanding public aid, shipper bias in favor of maximizing competition and certain regulatory policies have together brought about an ex-

---

[17] *Ibid.*, p. 322.
[18] *Ibid.*, p. 24.
[19] *Ibid.*, p. 26.

cessive number of carriers and overexpansion of transportation plant. They have set up trends which if continued unabated to 1975, will see private carriage rather than common carriage the base of the Nation's transportation system. The railroads, unable to adjust expenses to declining volume of business, may become government-owned. . . . Common carriers as we have known them are disappearing in water transportation and the highway common carriers are losing relative position and facing a prospect of higher operating ratios."[20]

The Doyle Report then summarizes its views as to improved organization of Federal regulatory and promotional activities. These proposals should be compared with Lloyd Wilson's recommendation in 1933 for establishment of one regulatory agency. The Doyle statements are as follows:

"The Civil Aeronautics Board, Interstate Commerce Commission and Federal Maritime Board should be consolidated into a single Federal Transportation Commission. . . . There should be a 'strong chairman'. . . . At top-staff echelons, the Commission should be organized by purpose [such as operating rights, rates, and services, etc.] for all modes, to avoid top-level organization by clientele [rail, air, highway, waterway and pipeline]. . . ."[21]

The Doyle report goes on to recommend a Department of Transportation. This is outlined in detail in Chapter IX[22]

The Doyle comments on railroad problems in 1961

Although one is 28 years older than the other, the Lloyd Wilson study published in 1933 and the 1961 Doyle Report both emphasize the adverse effect upon the railroads of the development of the other modes of transportation. Even in 1933 the railroads were no longer a monopoly, according to Professor Wilson. Both reports place major emphasis in explaining

---

[20] Eighty-seventh Congress, First Session, National Transportation Policy, Jan. 3, 1961, U.S. Government Printing Office, Washington, D.C.
[21] *Ibid.*, p. 11.
[22] *Ibid.*, pp. 11–12.

railroad difficulties upon the growth and effect of private carriage of both passengers and freight. And both urge merger of railroads as an important action that should be taken. The Wilson recommendation in favor of voluntary merger of the railroads "into a limited number of large systems" has been presented. The Doyle conclusions respecting merger are as follows:

> "General consolidation of railroads in the near future is presented as the most important measure to restore the railroad industry to the health and vigorous status of over 30 years ago and as a necessary basis for a coordinated transportation system for the Nation. . . . The public interest in maintaining privately owned railroads as a basic element of an efficient transportation system and one that will provide for economic growth and national defense requires early action. . . ."[23]

Differences and similarities, 1933 vs. 1961

This comparison of the Wilson study made by one distinguished scholar in 1933 and the recent 1961 Doyle report has revealed no important differences in approach or conclusions. Of course details differ. There are gaps in the earlier report due to the fact that some 1961 problems did not then exist. Absence of comment on carrying truck-trailers or van bodies on flat cars is an example of such a gap. The striking similarity of the two reports in identifying and analyzing major problems emphasizes how little change has taken place in the 28 years since 1933 in what was called then the Transportation Crisis and is called today the Transportation Problem.

The two reports do reveal that there has been a change in emphasis. To Lloyd Wilson in 1933 the entire transportation system was in jeopardy. We can understand this when we recall that common carriage was still the dominant transportation technique, and that the common carrier railroads were then relatively far more important than today.

The 1961 report also points to common carriage as being

---

[23] *Ibid.*, pp. 15–16.

threatened in future if not actually in jeopardy today. The Doyle study deals with common carriage as part of or as one phase of total transportation. The present-day and future importance of the three forms or techniques, contract, common, and private carriage, are thus placed in proper perspective. In its opening statement the Doyle report says that:

> "Our over-all system is not, at the moment, in acute financial distress, but there are strong indications of trouble ahead in the not too distant future. . . . All evidence points to the national necessity of preserving common carriage as the only means of providing the general transportation service needed by all."[24]

During the decade from 1942 through 1951 the stimulus of war and preparations for war greatly aided most of the common carriers, particularly the railroads. Between 1933 and 1961 railroads have gone through a period of high volume of traffic and of relatively high earnings. The World War II period has been followed by the declining railroad earnings trend of recent years. For some railroads the present traffic and earning levels have no counterpart except in the depression years before and after 1933. Average weekly carloads were 543,000 in 1933; and were 492,000 per week for the first quarter of 1961. This is another way of saying that the traffic lift given by World War II has now run its course.

The forces that had depressed the common carriers in 1933 were in 1961 again affecting the common carriers, particularly the railroads. These forces are competition from contract and private carriers; the effect of over-all excess transportation capacity which tends to be concentrated adversely against the common carriers; and unequal and unbalanced treatment of the different modes of transportation in matters of Federal promotion, taxation and regulation.

The Doyle report predicts that by 1975 the die will have been cast. Either common carriage performed by private enterprises will by then have been put on a sounder economic

---

[24] *Ibid.,* p. 1.

basis, as Lloyd Wilson urged in 1933, or, according to the Doyle prediction, the railroad common carriers will have been nationalized, and truck and water common carriers will either have disappeared or have lost their relative position.

It may be confidently assumed that in 1975 someone will issue a report on the Transportation Crisis of that year. Will this report again be an updating of the 1933 study? Will strong measures have been taken by Congress in the intervening years? In 1975, will the common carriers of that day have sufficient financial strength to make Government take-over unnecessary? Or will private carriage have become so dominant as to eliminate the need for common carriers whether owned by private enterprises or by the Government? Since we cannot foretell, let's just wait and see.

Chapter IV

AUDITING AND COST-DETERMINATION
AS LOGISTICS TOOLS

Before an enterprise can make its transportation choices, its management must make certain determinations through study and analysis of its needs and operations. There must be answered questions as to the nature, unit cost, and volume of each important traffic movement made directly or indirectly for the enterprise. The aim is to find and use the most desirable transportation, viewed not alone but as one of the numerous logistics factors. For this purpose the transportation audit is a powerful tool which should be in constant use regardless of the type of transportation involved.

TRANSPORTATION AUDITING

Transportation auditing is one type of internal auditing. Internal audits are now recognized as of much broader scope and importance than the mere inventory of assets and search for possible fraudulent or criminal acts by employees or outsiders. The purpose is not only to protect the assets of the enterprise but also to evaluate the effectiveness of use of tools, money, machines, and procedures. Internal audits are performed at irregular intervals. Each audit is limited in scope to one activity or "cost center." The usual result is a joint report by the manager and the auditor that corrective action has been worked out and put into effect.

For example, an audit of an inter-plant movement of semi-finished material by rail might show that two switching charges were being paid for in connection with most of the car movements. Investigation might pinpoint this as resulting from oral requests for "special movement service" by the loading foreman. Corrective action might be explanatory instructions to the loading foreman coupled with instructions not to pay switch charges unsupported by a written order.

The transportation type of internal audit is especially important in evaluating actual as well as prospective use of private carriage at frequent intervals. If recent trade publication articles are accurate in their reporting, some present-day traffic managers have become anxious to avoid any objective review or audit of their private carriage activities. The reason, it may be assumed, is that their decision to purchase or lease equipment and go into private transportation was either an initial error, or subsequently has become an error in judgment.

The logistics concept is based on use of mathematical thinking. If the facts underlying the reasoning were wrong to begin with or have changed, then such a situation should be audited. It must be dragged out in the "open" for review to arrive at a revised and corrected decision. According to such evidence as is available an initial decision to undertake private carriage often does become an error in judgment. A common reason is failure to include such overhead factors as the cost of money, the cost to the enterprise of services obtained from other departments, and the effect on total costs of seasonal or weekly under-usage of equipment and personnel. The case for transportation auditing of private carriage decisions is obvious.

Transportation auditing necessarily includes testing employee or executive performance regarding financial responsibility or honesty or accuracy in handling company matters; but it also and most importantly directs itself toward testing the controls exercised over the use made of transportation by the particular business for which the audit is being made. Transportation audits save money and make profits for any business that has substantial tonnage of inbound, outbound, and intra-plant movements or numerous shipments of any kind. They are an invaluable aid in accomplishment of one's business logistics objectives. This is because they provide information that corrects mistaken ideas or clarifies understanding, thus making discovery of the optimum pattern more certain.

Transportation auditing is, of course, not a substitute for the usual annual audit of corporation books and reports. It encompasses appreciation and understanding of the principles of cost accounting and, significantly, uses established cost standards as one of its tools in judging transportation performance. It is not methods engineering, although audit reports often help to reveal the need for procedural studies that lead to methods improvement, for example, by reduction of the costs and in the time required for repairs and maintenance.

Auditing of freight bills

Transportation auditing has been neglected in some corporations because the audit responsibility is divided. In many concerns the task is thought of as being primarily an audit of freight bills after payment. Usually this audit activity, together with processing of loss and damage claims, is handled by the traffic department. Traffic files and traffic department skill are both essential. However, this natural situation should not prevent the accounting department from performing other important audit tasks in the increasingly complex field of both purchased and private transportation, especially with respect to the logistical relations between transportation and other inbound assembly and outbound distribution factors.

Auditing of freight bills after payment is a necessity because of the certainty of some degree of human error. Furthermore, freight rate tariffs have been becoming more and more complex. Before World War II, in 1936, it was estimated that a skilled tariff rate analyst could ascertain a railroad freight rate in 3 to 5 minutes. He could then use this rate with confidence that there was no other applicable tariff item that might provide for a lower freight charge. Today the same skilled rate analyst will require from 9 to 15 minutes in which to read the same tariff and make needed calculations. Even then, the analyst will often be unable to assure himself that he has found and quoted the lowest applicable rate. His uncertainty will be due in part to the fact that, in addition to rail, numerous truck and barge tariffs must also be consulted. These complications are further increased by the effect of technological changes which have made partially obsolete the commodity descriptions and definitions upon which the applicability of freight rates must rely.

Post-audit of freight bills after payment usually results in refund of over-charges and filing of claims for loss or damage, ranging from 1 to 3 per cent of total freight charges originally paid, the recovery being greatest when the shipments are of varied character rather than being the same commodity from the same origin to the same destination. Clearly such recovery justifies and more than pays for this type of transportation audit.

However, the real value of freight bill post-auditing is in disclosure of opportunities for cost reduction. These are of several types. In some cases change in routing or selection of a different carrier may reduce cost or improve the service relationship to the other logistical factors. Often the post-audit will point to opportunities for advantageous private carriage. Audit of freight bills is, therefore, an important kind of transportation auditing. It will be even more useful when use of computer techniques makes possible the addition of equally accurate and complete pre-audit of cost and service alternatives before shipment.

Auditing of service practices

Carriers and/or government agencies have established increasingly rigid rules with respect to the safe maximum load that can be carried by each railroad car, truck, barge, vessel and aircraft. A shipper action that results in an overload may cause an accident. The resulting cost to the carrier can sometimes be charged back to the shipper. From self-interest, shippers should seek to avoid excessive overloads or unsafe loads. The resulting undue wear and the accidents that occur add to the total cost of for-hire transportation even when not recovered from the shipper or from the insurance carried by the shipper. Likewise from a selfish angle there are often good reasons to avoid underloading. When freight charges are on a per vehicle basis, or involve providing a stated minimum load per vehicle, underloading becomes additional transportation cost.

The transportation audit technique provides a practical and low-cost means of checking on actual management control of these important problems of overloading, unsafe loading, and/or underloading transportation equipment. Important direct and indirect savings can be brought about by its use for this purpose.

The five-day week immobilizes a large portion of the railroad freight cars and also of the local cartage and specialized industrial over-the-road trucks, for about one-fourth of each week. Any factor that adds further to this equipment wastage looms large. Such a factor is delay during the unloading and/or loading period, when the freight car or truck is being held subject to shipper or receiver actions and decisions. If the equipment is being operated in private carriage, the cost of delays and waiting is direct, yet is often buried in generalized reports. It can be "dug out" only by means of the audit technique.

Often trucks line up for blocks awaiting entry into a plant. They may then wait for hours within the plant. Clearly this problem of wasted transportation is not relieved by paying truck detention charges. The real cure is to lessen or eliminate the wastage of the time of trucks and their drivers. Here again transportation auditing can help to turn the spotlight on the details of the problem, and thus help to find a solution.

Auditing to reduce human error

Human error can result in carrier charges being paid when the movement did not occur, simply because of reliance upon oral understandings instead of written records. Habitual use of one method of transportation when a better and less costly one is readily available is another form of human error. For example, costly rail movements occur in congested or confined areas simply because all concerned are blind to other ways. Change to such equipment as straddle trucks or tank trucks may effect a substantial savings in cost and a significant improvement in transportation efficiency. Often the cost saving and service improvement pointed to by the transportation audit are attainable only by changing from use of a common or contract carrier to private carriage.

Another source of cost attributable to human error is in the loss of desired transit rights at some distant point, due to failure to place proper routing instructions on the bill of lading, or due to disregard of such routing instructions at the origin for some local and temporary reasons. Here again, the transportation audit is a valuable tool.

THE LOGISTICAL MATHEMATICS OF PRIVATE CARRIAGE EXEMPLIFIES COSTING TECHNIQUES

It is probable that most business ventures into private carriage have been initiated without knowledge of all the costs involved. Determination of cost, either before going into private carriage, or after operation has commenced is a task for trained accountants. Failure to obtain and to rely on carefully prepared accounting reports is a common reason for incorrect conclusions about cost.

Usually the initial estimates of the cost of private carriage are on the low side. For example, the enthusiastic proponent of private carriage often overlooks such elements as the cost of services such as light and heat, because obtained within the company. Also often forgotten is the fact that, if the capital investment was employed in buying a new production machine it would be expected to earn its share of administrative overhead and a profit as well as interest on investment. These accounting omissions can, of course, lead to errors in judgment. Costing techniques for evaluating private use of transportation equipment can be useful also in developing estimates of for-hire costs.

Lease versus purchase

An important decision preceding use of private carriage is as to the desirability of leasing or buying the equipment. By "lease" is meant not a legal instrument, but any financing procedure that provides for regular payments from current earnings, with the gradually declining unpaid balance guaranteed chiefly by the resale value of the particular equipment. The problem of an automobile for a salesman is a simple example of the choice that must be made in obtaining any kind of transportation equipment for private operation. The lease cost must be compared with the purchase costs of the car:

1. the price of the car,
2. interest on this money,
3. cost of supervision,
4. cost of maintenance,
5. *less* the net resale value.

Assume that net purchase *price* of an automobile delivered to a company salesman is $2400, that *supervision and clerical cost* incurred by the company during the life of this vehicle is $8, that the car is run 40,000 miles before turn-in at a cost for *fuel, tires,* and *repairs* of $1600, and that the car is sold after 24 months' use for a net yield of $800. The total cost, including interest at 4 per cent on the $2400 purchase price, is $3400.

Cost + Interest + Supervision + Operation and Maintenance − Resale Value
$2400 + $192 + $8 + $1600 − $800

Alternatively, the car may be leased. If 6 per cent interest is paid on the declining balance, with one thirty-sixth of the principal paid each month, interest will also be $192. $1600 of the original purchase price will have been paid out in two years. The sale price of $800 at the end of the two-year period equals the balance due so no adjustment is needed here. Cost of leasing the car, including $8 for supervision and clerical cost, and $1600 for fuel, tires and repairs would be $3400, the same as if it had been purchased. Whether the car is purchased or leased the cost would be 8.5 cents per mile of use.

The two examples of ownership versus leasing of a salesman's car have been equated by using a lower interest rate of 4 per cent for the company's total investment, and an interest rate of 6 per cent on the declining balance in the case of the leased car. This was done to illustrate that, often, the advantage of ownership versus leasing is dependent on assumptions that are deliberately favorable to ownership. In the case of interest, the fact that the company considered use of its own money was worth only 4 per cent does not justify purchase. The real question is what this money would return if it had been invested in a cost-reducing new machine for the company's factory. If the latter return is 10 per cent or even more, clearly the company's money should have gone into the new factory equipment and the salesman's car should have been leased.

There is an intangible value arising from leasing equipment for use in private transportation of either passengers or freight. This is that both lessor and lessee are interested in maintaining the leased automobiles or trucks or barges or railroad tank cars in good condition. There is less tendency to keep on using old equipment by making "makeshift repairs." The factor of clean, good looking and well-maintained vehicles can be valuable as a contribution to safety, morale, public relations and advertising. Of great importance is its effect in encouraging careful and efficient use of the equipment.

This intangible factor can become an offset to the fact that leasing, by introducing a second corporation which must be paid for its services, tends to cost slightly more than direct ownership. Of course such a comparison that is slightly adverse to leasing is valid only if one assumes that both lessor and lessee can obtain funds for their equipment capital requirements at the same interest rate. Even if this is the case it is not valid if the money used for purchase could have earned a substantially higher return, for example, by being invested in additional production facilities or in a new or more efficient warehouse.

The effect of the estimated load factor

The key question that determines whether to undertake private carriage of one's own freight is whether operating efficiency can be developed and maintained by the private operator. If the load factor is inadequate, for example, the unit cost will be high. There will be little or no justification for private carriage, unless positively required because of the favorable effect on other logistical factors.

Assume the capacity of one tractor-trailer is 17 tons per trip. It can make 250 round trips (or 500 one-way trips) per year between the factory and a warehouse located 200 miles away. From plant to warehouse it is known that the load will vary from 10 tons minimum to 17 tons maximum and will average 12 tons. On the return trip, the average is to be 2 tons. The annual lift will be 3500 tons, while the annual capacity is 8500 tons. Thus the load factor is 41 per cent.

Whether use of a company-operated private truck with over half of its capacity unused is justified depends on part on the tangible and intangible advantages of having full control of operation. One tangible advantage may be reduction in the cost of packaging, since the truck body can be designed to protect unpackaged or lightly packaged products. Another is the ability to schedule the truck so as to eliminate the need to hold reserve inventory at the warehouse. These small savings can be measured by skilled accountants, and their dollar value estimated.

Of greater importance may be the intangible service feature that the private truck can make deliveries under emergency conditions direct to the customer, thus by-passing the warehouse. Or the truck may take part of its freight in a container which is transferred to a local truck at an intermediate point for delivery to customers. While such service may be duplicated by common carriers, its additional cost must be paid for. The company's own truck can perform much of this type of special customer service with little or no addition to its cost, provided use of private carriage has already been found desirable and justified by the regular movements and despite the low load factor.

There is an obvious relation between the degree of decentralization of production and consumption and the need for private carriage of freight. Viewing the century that has elapsed since mechanized transportation by railroad, steamboat, and pipeline became an important *agent of industrialization,* decentralization has shown rapid and continuing growth. At the time of the American Civil War, Great Britain was the major industrial nation. Raw materials flowing toward England and industrial products moving in the opposite direction helped to shape the East-West pattern for American common carriers by railroad.

The industrial New England and North Atlantic states gradually supplanted the formerly dominant British manufacturers. This shortened the raw material and finished products hauls, and became the first step toward decentralization.

Today industry of all types is established in all the numerous economic regions within the United States. The national market has thus been sub-divided into numerous smaller markets. As a result inbound and outbound hauls are, on the average, much shorter than a century ago. This reduction in length of haul has been a major factor that has stimulated and justified much of the great increase in private carriage, particularly by truck. The higher per-mile charges made by common carriers for short distances combined with the service flexibility of private carriage by truck, usually offset the low load factor.

Despite the obvious relation between decentralization and private carriage, there is no single pattern that will automatically guide decision. To treat this relationship as a generalization applicable to all situations is unsound and will only lead to costly errors. Each private carriage situation must be tested and evaluated in its own environment. Furthermore, the old adage that "one man's meat may be another man's poison" aptly describes the fact that competing users of transportation may need private carriage in different ways.

One petroleum refiner may rely on common carrier pipelines. Another may own and operate a fleet of private barges. One chain store concern may have its own private trucks deliver to stores in one direction, then haul products from a factory to a central distributing warehouse in the reverse direction. A competing chain store enterprise may use railroad common carriers to deliver products from factories to numerous local warehouses from which distribution to the retail stores is accomplished by contract truck. In these examples the average load factor is one of the basic determinants as to whether or not to engage in private carriage.

Computing average transit time

Private carriage is most useful and low in cost when circumstances permit a high-average load factor. Equally important is ability to keep all of the equipment in constant use. The natural tendency of private carriage is to accumulate more equipment than is desirable from the standpoint of both optimum service and cost. This problem of determining the best relation between equipment and tonnage ready for shipment can be approached from two different angles. Both require a survey to determine the over-all time required for an average round trip, including the loading and unloading intervals.

Assume that the trips made by one truck in a week average out at five hours, broken down into 45 minutes for loading, an equal time for unloading, and 210 minutes time in transit on the round trip. The five-hour period required for the average trip means that only one trip can be accomplished per 8-hour day. This is a practical or empirical estimate based on the fact that an average is composed of actual situations, some of which will greatly exceed or fall short of the five-hour average. The cost of overtime operates as a penalty against any effort to make two trips in one 8-hour shift. Another factor is that, in making deliveries either to a customer or to one's own warehouse or plant, it is undesirable to arrive at destination less than two hours before the end of the normal work day. This is to avoid imposing overtime costs upon the receiver of the truck shipment. This consideration also immobilizes both for-hire, and private carriage delivery by truck on Saturdays, Sundays, and holidays.

If the average time of five hours is divided into 40 hours, the theoretical number of trips in a normal work week would be eight. As shown, the minimum that can be estimated realistically is five trips per week. On the five-trip basis the utilization is 62½ per cent of the theoretical maximum. Combined with a load factor of say 25 per cent (average one-way load using half the capacity of the truck, returning empty), there may be little or no cost-saving justification for use of private carriage.

Determining equipment requirements

Many transportation situations require use of more than one truck, or barge, or airplane, or freight car. Cost competitiveness of private carriage requires favorable utilization of equipment capacity. Achievement of low cost of private transportation requires decision as to the optimum number of vehicles needed for a particular movement.

Assume a situation such as

Volume to move:	500 tons per day, 50 weeks per year, 5 hours round-trip time, 5-day week
Capacity of each truck:	20 tons per one-way trip
Investment and operating cost per truck:	$ 8,500 to $10,000 per year according to use
Driver earnings and related costs:	$10,000 per year
Loading and unloading helper, cost per man:	$ 6,000 per year

There are three possible ways to supply 500 tons per day by truck with in-transit time, including loading and unloading time, of five hours per round trip. The entire 500 tons can be moved in a single 8-hour shift. This will require 25 trucks and the same number of drivers, but only two loading-unloading helpers. On a two-shift basis, by careful scheduling, three trips by nine trucks can be made in 16 hours without overtime penalties, requiring four helpers. On a three-shift basis it becomes possible to schedule four trips by seven trucks, using six helpers.

The single shift operation would require:

25 trucks costing $8,500 each $212,500
25 drivers costing $10,000 each 250,000
2 helpers costing $6,000 each 12,000

$474,500

average cost per ton: 474,500 ÷ 125,000 = $3.796

A two-shift operation, with three trips per day per truck would require:

9 trucks costing $9,500 each ....$ 85,500
18 drivers costing $10,000 each 180,000
4 helpers costing $6,000 each 24,000

$289,500

average cost per ton: 289,500 ÷ 125,000 = $2.316

A three-shift operation with four trips per day per truck would take:

7 trucks costing $10,000 each ....$ 70,000
21 drivers costing $10,000 each 210,000
6 helpers costing $6,000 each 36,000

$316,000

average cost per ton: 316,000 ÷ 125,000 = $2.528

In this example the most desirable operation plan appears to be the two-shift arrangement, requiring nine trucks, 18 drivers, and four helpers for loading and unloading. (It should be noted that this example has been greatly simplified to bring out the fundamental factors.

The complexity of private carriage logistics

These simple examples may seem to belabor the obvious. In fact, they represent the type of analysis that is essential to sound decision-making but that is often omitted. Furthermore, such analysis should be repeated at intervals if the enterprise is to remain in an optimum position in its use of private carriage, and in its evaluation of existing or proposed freight rates.

It must also be borne in mind that these examples all deal with transportation as the major factor to be considered. As has been shown in other chapters, this is rarely the case. Other factors such as warehouse location and operation and convenience in delivery to customers also must be incorporated into the logistical analysis. The mathematics required for decision then becomes complex indeed.

> *Cost analysis as a tool of transportation management is not as impervious to change as it may at times appear to be. . . . Recently, for instance, containerization has generated increased interest . . . in the relationship of "number of pieces" to handling costs. . . . Contrary to some current thought, a great share of so-called constant and joint costs are neither unfathomable nor indivisible and may be reasonably and effectively traced, measured and managed . . . the increased willingness on the part of management and policy makers to accept a greater degree of sophistication and complexity in cost analysis may be described as one beneficial side effect of the "computer age." [Quoted from article by Dr. K. P. Rahbany, Traffic World Magazine, October 6, 1962, Washington, D.C., pages 60 and 72.]*

Chapter V

PACKAGING FOR SHIPMENT, SECUREMENT OF LADING, CONTAINERIZATION AND WAREHOUSING

In all aspects of business logistics, it is necessary to avoid overemphasis on current technical detail. The true emphasis must be on the concept of optimum adjustment, not only in the present, but also in relation to future developments to the extent they can be foreseen and included in planning.

Milk offers an apt example. In some countries goat's milk still is transported in its original container, that is, the animal. The goat is driven by its owner to the customer's door and the milk is then transferred from the animal to the container provided by the purchaser. Not too different was the early practice in the United States of the small dairy farmer who supplied his own family and half a dozen customers. As he made his rounds he delivered milk by pouring out of his own 10-gallon can into customer-provided pitchers or pails.

Gradually in America delivery of milk to users became a business in itself, sometimes but not necessarily related to the dairy farm or farms. Concepts of cleanliness, uniformity of quantity measurement, and ease of delivery led to the returnable and reusable glass bottle. Today the glass bottle has been replaced by the disposable square container made of treated cardboard. This change took place in part because of the need for weight reduction, in part because it was more sanitary, and perhaps in part because it is easier for the consumer to handle and carry away from the supermarket. The square shape also saved space in shipment and storage, even in the customer's refrigerator.

The trend away from delivery of milk to the customer's door and towards purchase at a store eliminates some distribution expense, thus permitting a slightly lower retail price. Actually, the customer, by using his own automobile, has incurred some delivery expense. This is of little importance to him compared to his personal convenience.

Much research effort has been aimed toward finding out how to preserve milk for indefinite periods of time by some sort of "canning" process. If and when this effort is successful, delivery of fresh milk direct to the customer may disappear entirely. Furthermore, it will become possible to ship and warehouse milk like any canned goods item.

This milk delivery illustration shows that packaging is constantly evolving in response to factors that include but are not limited to transportation. Logistics procedures and methods of thinking would not be necessary if there were only one or two variables to consider in arriving at the best answer. Among the many factors involved are cost of the package; its reusability; its contribution toward extending the time before spoilage of contents begins; warehouse possibilities and cost; customer preference; effect on transportation conditions and cost; and future technical or marketing developments.

Relation of packaging to securement, containerization and warehousing

Securement of lading for transportation is interrelated with packaging. It is also affected by the design of the cargo-carrying space or spaces of the particular vehicle or vessel. The need for securement and its nature varies from mode to mode. Both are also affected by the manner of operation, especially the effects of high speed and of deceleration shocks.

Securement of lading is entirely a transportation cost. On the other hand the cost of packaging may be of "joint" nature. For example, part of the packaging cost may be incurred for marketing reasons leaving only a portion directly attributable to transportation. Some of this transportation-caused portion of packaging cost usually is due to the necessity to arrange the individual packages in groups, by crating or boxing or containerization, so as to reduce the cost or increase the effectiveness of securement.

Containerization is related to both packaging and securement. This is particularly likely to be the case where containers can be transferred from one mode to another, as from rail to vessel, without opening or damaging their contents. Containerization has other advantages such as reducing or eliminating pilferage. Containers may become temporary warehouses at destination, a possibility that becomes important in wartime. They may be loaded with odd-shaped packages or with packages so frail that they would be crushed if not protected by the container walls and roof. Containers may be made watertight for liquids. When made gastight, different atmospheric conditions in the interior than outside can be maintained during transport. They may, of course, be heated or refrigerated. Their availability in various sizes further increases adaptability to user needs. Containers may be made inexpensively so as to be thrown away at destination; or made collapsible for empty return if back-haul lading is not available.

Packaging and securement practices affect warehouse design and procedures. Properly designed and coordinated warehouses can result in optimum packaging and securement requirements and lower unit costs. The aim of business logistics, to achieve the best relation between cost and customer convenience, is best accomplished when packaging, securement, containerization and warehousing are viewed as different but interrelated facets of the same problem.

Packaging for shipment and sale

Packaging involves both marketing and logistics considerations. These include appearance, convenience, ease of assembly into a wholesale or retail unit of sale when required, protection from damage, achievement of lowest possible unit cost of the packaging operation, and provision for efficient warehousing.

The term "packaging" naturally calls to mind the package or wrapper designed for some food product as it is displayed in a store. In fact everything that is made and sold is "packaged" during part or all of its journey between the finishing operations and actual usage by a customer. Thus packaging in this broad sense can mean assembly of bulk commodities in customary quantities.

An example is liquid sugar in tanks, sugar in sacks, or fiber boxes filled with 100 one-pound cardboard containers of sugar. Packaging can also mean the assembly of 25 corrugated bars, for use in reinforcement of concrete, into a "bundle" or "lift" by means of "strapping." It can mean the fiber box in which a new television set or living room chair is delivered by a department store. These examples show that the term "packaging" covers every device or method of grouping or arranging products for convenient handling during the interval between production and delivery to a customer.

The same product may be "packaged" in several different ways. Thus if a can of food complete with an attractive wrapper is a package, so also is the fiber box containing 24 or 48 of the cans. If, for convenience in warehousing and subsequent shipment, three of the fiber boxes are then fastened to a "pallet" or "skid," this three-box unit also is a package. If 30 of the three-box units are then loaded into a container, it too can be thought of as a package. This illustration shows that the packaging engineer, interested in finding optimum solutions for his logistics problems, often finds it desirable to place packages within packages.

The packaging engineer seeks to plan both the outer and inner packages for good appearance and for convenient handling by the receiver. Good appearance not only connotes quality; it promotes quality by delivering a product that looks usable because it is in good condition. Of course good appearance includes the artistic or advertising uses of the outside of the package, as well as necessary directions or information.

Convenient handling by the final or ultimate customer is the reason for relatively small size of the inner package. It is intended to protect a quantity of product, often one item only, adapted to user need. The outer package usually protects and holds together a number of items or individual inner packages. It may be thought of as a wholesale-type of package. The quantity it contains must be compatible with the commercial practices of the particular industry. In addition, this type of package must be convenient to handle in the warehouse. It must be easy to fill, seal, store and unload.

Until recently the wooden crate, box or barrel as the outer or wholesale-type package for merchandise was used almost universally. The use of wooden packages sometimes was proof of traditional thinking. In other words, progress in packaging has in recent years seemed to require use of other materials such as fiberboard or heavy paper or plastic or metal. However, such criticism of wood is unfair, since the real fault often has been with design of the package. Where weight saving is not a major factor, wooden packages have an important place. For example, in ocean transportation stowage problems are simplified when the packages are of wood, even though of different sizes. Wood has elasticity. Its contact with the metal deck and with other boxes provides adhesion and permits controlled sliding.

Package appearance, convenience, and commercial compatibility are all important, but worthless if there is not also protection from damage during warehousing and transit. All four of these technical factors may be found in a particular package; yet the packaging method must be discarded if the same results can be obtained at lower unit cost in some other way.

Evolution of cooperative approach to packaging

Evolution has taken place not only in variety of packaging materials and methods, but also in the attitude of shippers, receivers and carriers. Less than two centuries ago, carriers considered that all responsibility for proper packaging to protect against damage in transit lay with the shipper. Related to this attitude toward damage was the fact that carrier equipment was designed essentially for the performance of the carriage function alone. In the distant past no effort was made to design carrier's equipment to lessen or eliminate transportation damage. Ships' holds, in the days of wooden vessels, were damp and shaped to conform to the narrow and curved outer hull. Animal-drawn vehicles and barges were usually little more than open platforms. The small dimensions of vehicles and barges, combined with the limits on size and weight caused by use of human strength in loading and unloading, forced use of relatively small outer packages. These had to be of sturdy and solid wood for boxes and barrels, or of strong cloth for bags or bales. In either case the ratio of weight and cost of packaging to the weight and value of the contents was high.

The contrast between the 18th century packaging and transportation interrelation and that of today is striking. The carrier and receiver now have become cooperating partners in the task of eliminating in-transit loss and damage. Mere increase in the size and weight-carrying capacity of carrier equipment such as trucks, freight cars, barges, vessels and airplanes has itself been an important factor. Larger outer packages are thus made possible with resulting reduction in the ratio of packaging weight and cost to the product's weight and value. Many articles formerly shipped as parts can now be shipped fully assembled and ready for use. This reduces transit damage since parts are more subject to loss or to lessening of usefulness when not held securely in place in the finished product.

In addition to providing larger freight-carrying spaces in equipment, carriers have become more expert in designing such spaces for their functional uses. Refrigeration is an example. Providing heat within exacting limitations is another. Arranging dimensions so that large outer packages, or containers, are easily loaded and shipped is important. Providing improved devices to absorb shocks is of very great value, since it permits use of higher speed with lessened instead of increased damage.

SECUREMENT OF LADING IN CARRIER EQUIPMENT

Less than ten years ago, the dramatic change-over from steam to diesel locomotives was at its peak. As this change-over progressed new factors affecting securement of lading for rail shipments became painfully evident. The new problems and their solution illustrate the evolution of carrier-user cooperation.

During and immediately after World War II, the diesel change-over consisted almost entirely in mingling road-haul steam and diesel locomotives. There was little diesel switching. This meant that operating practices as to road-haul speed and avoidance of damage-causing switching impacts were, during this interim, derived from the steam locomotive. Under such conditions the diesel locomotive seemed to promise reduction in transit damage.

Yard switching diesels, as compared with steam switch engines, are less able to avoid severe coupling impacts at more than six miles per hour. Diesels often couple at eight or ten miles per hour. In addition increased use of hump switching yards, to save locomotive and yard labor expense as well as time, has increased the frequency of violent impacts between freight cars.

As we now know, the diesel locomotive does cause damage to freight, particularly when merchandise is loaded in older freight cars that were reasonably satisfactory when steam hauled.

When a freight train more than a mile long is traveling at 60 miles per hour behind a giant diesel locomotive, portions of the train will be in different positions on the track's undulations and curves. If the engineer uses his brakes in accordance with the undulation and curve conditions just ahead of the engine, this brake use will have quite different effects in back of him. The air-brake pressure travels slowly so that brakes tend to be applied or released in sequence from locomotive to caboose. There is engineered into each freight car a "slack action" of a few inches, that becomes many feet at the caboose, as 100 or more freight cars close up against the locomotive, or vice versa.

The first reaction of railroad executives to increased road-haul shocks and switching impacts was to seek to "beef up" requirements for packaging of merchandise and for securement of lading. However it speedily became evident that shippers neither could nor would provide at their own expense packaging and securement that would be so adequate, as was facetiously remarked, that the package could be dropped onto pavement from a third-story window without damage to contents. This shipper inability to provide additional protection stems only in part from the additional cost of stronger packages, more dunnage, and more effective cargo-holding and shock-absorbing devices.

There are important differences in the commercial practices of railroads and common carrier truck and barge operators with respect to payment, need and responsibility for securement of lading. These differences have become of competitive importance between the modes.

When loading a barge, the shipper or his agent places the cargo so that its weight is evenly distributed. No securement is needed or used. Hence, there is no cost to the shipper or receiver of freight.

When loading a truck, the shipper or his agent places the packages or "lifts" as directed by the driver who is the carrier's agent. The driver then secures the lading, when considered necessary, by means of chains equipped with turnbuckles that can be tightened. As far as the shipper or receiver is concerned there is no cost for securement of lading.

On the other hand, when loading a railroad flat car or gondola car with merchandise, the shipper must comply at his own expense with prescribed loading rules. These are exacting in their requirements as to how to secure the lading to the car. Usually these rules are designed to permit the lading to slide under control of wooden guides and buffers made of dunnage, and of a device called a "brake." All material and labor is supplied by and paid for by the shipper. The purpose is to convert the impact shocks into a controlled sliding effect. Shippers have been reluctant to bear increased securement of lading cost, and have often turned to use of other modes that do not have such requirements.

Within the last few years railroads have begun to redesign their freight cars to meet the new conditions. This effort has taken two directions, piggy-back and damage-free cars.

Damage-free freight cars are designed so that the entire platform on which the lading has been piled or stacked "floats" on the sub-structure of the car. This floating or sliding of the entire car floor is controlled in various ways. In some designs the freight-carrying platform may slide as much as three feet and then return to its normal equal distance from the couplers at each end. The lading is lightly but firmly fixed to the floor of such cars by various means, including permanent fixtures or "dunnage" supplied by the railroad as part of the car. The lading itself is no longer intended or expected to slide, since the entire car floor performs that function. This redesign not only meets the problem of increased impact shocks but also transfers the cost of protecting the lading from shipper to carrier. It has permitted the railroad to approximate the securement of lading situation achieved by barge or truck.

The relation of piggy-back to packaging and securement

Up to this point little consideration has been given to the receiver. The chief point already made is that his interest is in receiving packages of the wholesale or retail type, or both, that contain quantities convenient in a commercial sense. These packages must be adapted to his warehouse or his storage shelves.

One of the minor but vital packaging and securement factors is the cost and annoyance involved in unloading. When an empty freight car has to be sent to a "cleaning track" by a railroad, usually it is because it is filled with unloading debris such as dunnage, steel strapping, heavy paper used as a tarpaulin over the load, and sometimes the outer fiber or wooden crate or box materials. The receiver has gone to considerable expense to remove these outer layers; he has reduced his annoyance by leaving them as debris in the empty car instead of trucking them to his own refuse dump.

Use of piggy-back by the shipper eliminates much of this unloading and unpackaging problem of the receiver. Trucks do not need heavy wholesale-type packaging or additional materials for weather protection and securement of lading. Furthermore when it is riding on a railroad flat car the rubber tires of the trailer help to absorb impact shocks just as they do when rolling over a highway.

Another advantage of piggy-back is in reaching beyond the team-track or the plant railroad siding to the optimum unloading point. This may be right next to the factory machine that takes the material for further processing. The final off-rail distance may be as short as fifty feet. However, if the merchandise is not trucked over-the-road or handled by piggy-back on a flat car, this final truck haul, whether short or long, can be both costly and annoying. Hence piggy-back helps railroads to compete with over-the-road truck transportation by providing the receiver with the unloading convenience of trucking as well as competitive unloading cost.

IDENTIFICATION OF PACKAGES DURING STORAGE AND TRANSIT

Three systems of "package," or "lift," or "lot" identification are in general use. These are use of a written tag or label, identification by location and self-identification. Of course use of the written tag or label is centuries old. So is identification by location in the warehouse or ship; this method is having a kind of revival as a result of increased containerization of merchandise. Self-identification of each package is new and seems to have great potential as well as present usefulness.

Combinations of all three methods are in common use. The now-familiar use of magnetic ink symbols on personal checks is an apt example. When the check is presented at the cashier's window, the written portions serve for identification. Subsequently the checks are sorted by banks, are mailed as a lot or group and the total value of all checks issued against accounts in one bank becomes a bookkeeping item. While in transit the checks, thus sorted and mailed to one bank, are identified by location, i.e., the envelope that contains them. At the bank where the account is located the checks are sorted by means of the self-identifying magnetic ink symbols, so that all the checks to be posted as withdrawals from one particular depositor's account are together. This oversimplified description of the complexities of bank "checking account" bookkeeping shows how all three methods of identification are used together, each in the manner that contributes most to optimum accuracy and lowest cost.

When a food product is being placed in cans, the machine operator visually ascertains that the fiber cartons he is filling carry words that describe the product. Each fiber box also carries a distinctive code. After each box has been filled and closed by the machine, it moves by conveyor into the plant's warehouse. The box stays on the conveyor until it identifies itself by means of the code. This act of self-identification then trips devices that shift the box onto a side conveyor. From here it may go into a truck or freight car. More often it goes onto a storage pile in the warehouse. In this "pile," or "bay" or "aisle," it becomes one of many boxes with like contents and is here identified by location.

Common carriers by truck or rail, also forwarders and express or parcel-delivery companies, have been inventive in the use of containers to minimize the problem of identification of packages during transit. An example is the development of "all-commodity" freight rates that encourage a shipper to assemble his small package shipments for one destination until he has enough for economical use of a small container. He loads this container at origin such as New York, and unloads it at destination such as Los Angeles. The container carries its proper written label and perhaps also its self-identification code. The packages themselves are identified only by location, that is, they are in the container.

The logical goal is self-identification of the "wholesale-type" package, small or large, during its entire service as protective cover, convenient and efficient storage unit and damage-free in-transit package. Many minds are grappling with this problem. Success in the fairly near future seems assured.

FEWER FREIGHT CARS WILL BE NEEDED IN THE FUTURE

A few decades ago there were over 2 million freight cars owned and operated by the railroads. Now there are 1⅔ million. If the current high number and per cent of bad order cars is subtracted there are about 1½ million usable vehicles. This downward trend seems certain to continue. By 1999, there will probably be about 1 million railroad-owned freight cars on United States railroads. Of course, this fleet of freight cars, though reduced in number, will be relatively new and will consist of larger cars that will be better designed for traffic needs than is true of today's freight cars. The same trend toward increase in size and reduction in number of pieces of transportation equipment required to perform a given movement task is found in all the modes.

As the number of freight cars is reduced, the need for greater utilization of each unit increases. Otherwise rail freight transportation will slump, whereas even the most conservative estimates are that rails will hold their own in volume but not in per cent of inter-city freight as our nation grows larger. The needed greater utilization must come not only from larger freight cars, but also from better railroad operation and better utilization by shippers.

Partly in response to the change in vehicle size the number of carloadings have dropped nationally by about 29 per cent since 1951. A drop of over 39 per cent has occurred on the eastern railroads during the same period, in part due to shipper use of forwarders, trucks and containers. Railroads out-

TRENDS IN CARLOADINGS

Year	All Railroads	Railroads other than Eastern	Eastern Railroads
1951............	40,499,000	21,991,000	18,508,000
1952............	37,985,000	21,301,000	16,684,000
1953............	38,216,000	21,238,000	16,978,000
1954............	33,915,000	19,661,000	14,254,000
1955............	37,636,000	21,127,000	16,509,000
1956............	37,845,000	21,173,000	16,672,000
1957............	35,500,000	19,852,000	15,648,000
1958............	30,222,000	18,063,000	12,159,000
1959............	31,015,000	18,427,000	12,588,000
1960............	30,441,000	18,229,000	12,212,000
1961............	28,584,000	17,377,000	11,207,000

side of eastern territory show a decline of about 21 per cent. There has been a partially offsetting gain in tons of freight carried in the average car. In 1943 this average was 41.0 tons per car; by 1960 this had increased to 44.4 tons, a gain of eight per cent.

Another facet of the equipment utilization problem brings into focus the extent to which a freight car is used to move goods from one place to another. Consider the picture as shown by figures compiled by the Interstate Commerce Commission.

Year	Freight Train Speed	Car Miles Per Active Car Day	Hours Per Day Standing or Moving in Terminals
1920	10.3	27.2	21.4
1930	13.8	38.6	21.2
1940	16.7	42.2	21.5
1950	16.8	47.4	21.2
1960	19.5	46.0	21.6

Train speeds have about doubled since 1920 and car-miles per car-day have increased in a smaller proportion. But while this was taking place, cars continued to stand on customer sidings or move around in the terminals almost 90 per cent of their time. It is surprising that the average car only performed over-the-road transportation service for about three hours each day in 1920; and it is alarming that it is doing about the same in 1960.

Innovations in handling non-bulk freight are developing

Carload traffic of all kinds does not need assembly in the long maximum-tonnage freight trains desirable for carrying bulk commodities. We can visualize a rail line having an average traffic of 75 carloads of non-bulk freight in one direction daily. The desirability of holding this traffic to assemble into a 225-car train once every three days is not going to be determined by railroad operating economies. If much of the non-bulk carload traffic can be moved by truck, this competitive fact will force retention of the daily freight train. Actually, many railroads have found it necessary and desirable to increase their freight train frequency, running shorter trains, in order to compete with trucks.

There is a pathway of cooperation for railroads and shippers that will reduce unit costs and improve service over that now given to carload freight. Railroad trends are already evident: toward piggy-back flat cars and toward handling all types of freight cars in scheduled, fast freight trains. Shipper preferences also are clear. Where practicable, shippers will use the full lading capacity of each freight car in return for reduced freight rates made possible by one of the several incentive plans or systems of rate-making. Users will provide efficient utilization conditions for specially designed freight cars in order to get the cars back as soon as possible for another load. And, where given the opportunity, shippers are using piggy-back service to an extent that forecasts the disappearance of the unspecialized, so-called "all-purpose" box car.

Shipper-carrier cooperation is the key

What else can shippers do? They can encourage the trend in new car building toward freight cars which are larger in maximum payload, and, where desirable, in cubic capacity or floor area. They can analyze and adjust their facilities so as to make the most effective use of such equipment, bearing in mind the economic advantages to themselves both in inter-city freight costs and in handling of freight in their plants. Also shippers can cooperate with railroads to improve car turnaround by faster loading and by faster and cleaner unloading.

It is important that rail carriers learn to transfer freight cars from one to another with less delay, and, it should be added, less cost to themselves. To help carriers accomplish this, shippers must become more understanding of railroad problems. For example, it is not an act of helpful cooperation for shippers to prescribe routing intended to slow down freight cars and thereby add to carrier costs.

Roughly 18 per cent of all freight cars are held for over 48 hours for loading and unloading. How many trucks would be available today for outbound shipments if shippers made a practice of holding them, in many cases with the drivers, in excess of 48 hours for loading and unloading? From the narrow point of view, many traffic men and distribution executives seem to think of the common carriers only as a standby facility always ready to furnish the equipment to be loaded at the industry's convenience. These same users fully expect to load or unload their own truck or container promptly. Perhaps even greater use of piggy-back and over-the-road trucking is the answer, since such user-choices save car-days simply by failing to use box cars. In general, flat cars used for piggy-back movement of trailers show high utilization. This example of evolution in freight car utilization shows again, from a quite different angle, the importance of trucks and of containers.

WAREHOUSE DESIGN CONSIDERATIONS

The term package has been used in the broad sense of every form in which retail and wholesale quantities of merchandise are handled between the factory and the final recipient. Warehouse is the term commonly used to describe the covered or open space where merchandise is held prior to initial shipment or at some point intermediate between factory and consumer. The three terms, packaging, warehousing, and outbound transportation together are often identified as "physical distribution."

All these are logistics terms or concepts. From the standpoint of the product itself, there is no exact line of demarcation between the physical distribution of merchandise and the storage and transportation of dry and liquid bulk products. Bulk products are chiefly of raw material nature; that is, their final destination is a factory-type enterprise where they are used in the process of making something such as electric energy, railroad transportation, or merchandise. Thus, sugar may be in merchandise form when in five-pound retail cartons; or in liquid or dry bulk form, when in a tank truck being transported to a large bakery or a candy factory.

A warehouse is much more than a place where shelter or heat or cold or humidification is provided to the extent needed.

The basic or original reason for warehousing was to protect merchandise against deterioration, theft, or the hazard of being mislaid or forgotten.

Four additional factors of logistical nature also must be considered in making decisions on design, location and operation of warehouses. First, each must be located so that in-and-out transportation conditions and costs are optimum, that is, the best attainable. Second, each must be designed for optimum handling and rehandling conditions and costs within the warehouse. Third, the provisions made for seasonal or other surge situations must be compatible with and not upsetting to normal warehouse operations. Fourth, paperwork necessary for inventory control and scheduling of inbound materials and of newly manufactured merchandise destined for storage or for outbound shipment, must be accurate, timely and as low in cost as possible. These three, location, internal design for normal and surge operation conditions, and efficient paperwork, must be effectively interrelated. And warehousing activities must in turn be compatible with retail and wholesale packaging needs, as well as with selection of the best of the numerous transportation alternatives.

Locating the warehouses

Warehouse locations are of two types, "close-to-factory" and "close-to-user." They may also be described as primary and secondary, or as plant warehouse and wholesale-type warehouses. For convenience the terms primary and secondary will be used. Where the market area is very large, there may be numerous secondary warehouses. Large multiple-plant manufacturing concerns also will have as many primary warehouses as there are separate factories. Again for convenience one primary and numerous secondary warehouses will be assumed.

The ideal location for the primary warehouse is the one that permits merchandise to be finished, packaged, moved to the warehouse and then moved within the warehouse to its assigned location as one continuous, automatic operation. It follows that this location must be as close to the factory-finishing operations as possible, otherwise conveyor length will become unduly costly.

The ideal locations for the secondary warehouses can only be determined by logistical reasoning based on analysis of data covering all of the interrelated aspects of the problem. These include location and relative importance of customers on a product-by-product basis; increase in sales volume due to delivery from a near-by point instead of from the primary warehouse; and cost of shipment in large volume from primary to secondary warehouse versus the cost of shipping smaller quantities from the primary warehouse directly to the customer.

The mathematical device known as linear programming is useful in determining proper location of secondary warehouses. The procedure in linear programming is to choose, by means of mathematics, an optimum combination of transportation, inventory ownership and warehouse costs. This mathematics device picks one such minimum combination of costs. By comparing costs from several assumed locations, the best location for a particular secondary warehouse is indicated.

Mathematical analysis of alternative secondary warehouse locations often leads to discovery of habitual errors in judgment. For example, the optimum cost may depend in part on increase in the volume of each shipment from primary to secondary warehouse, with resulting increase in the number of small shipments from the secondary point back toward the primary point. An irregular or even changeable boundary between two secondary warehouses may lead to the lowest over-all unit cost, due to the size and location of particular customers. Renting numerous small warehouse spaces at different locations may provide less costly and better customer delivery service than a delivery from a smaller number of large and well-equipped secondary warehouses. The logistical problems of each geographical area and of each of the larger customers are unique. Solutions that are right today may become wrong tomorrow. One of the gains from increased attention in recent years to "physical distribution" has been to emphasize the importance of constant review of both location and use of secondary warehouses.

Warehouse stock control

An unfortunate characteristic of all warehouses is that the most recent packages, or "lifts," or "lots," or "containers" are always on top of the assigned pile or stack. To minimize this, the normal practice is to have at least two piles or stacks at the assigned location in the warehouse. While one is being gradually shipped out, the other is being built up.

It is fortunate that production scheduling often is performed by the same executives who are responsible for the primary warehouse. This permits direct coordination of the internal warehouse operation of stacking and unstacking with the arrival of newly produced merchandise.

It is customary to establish maximum and minimum inventory levels, particularly in primary warehouse control of production and receipt of newly manufactured merchandise. Somewhere in between is the "order point," or signal to schedule a new production run of the particular commodity. This rather primitive system should be and is being replaced by a more complex approach that permits consideration of numerous logistics factors. These include the cost of owning and storing packaged merchandise including losses due to spoilage or damage; the effect upon cost of warehousing of varying use of space due to seasonal variation in sale of particular products; the cost or loss when shortage of inventory causes a customer to give his order to some other concern; the extra cost of making emergency delivery by means such as air freight. This may save an order that otherwise might be lost. Another factor is the excess in unit production cost if production runs are scheduled in quantities less than required for most efficient machine operation.

Usually there are only two key variables in determining the size of the next production run of a particular product, when production is scheduled to keep the primary warehouse inventory in balance. These are the range of unit costs due to scheduling production of less than or more than the most efficient quantity and the range of the combined unit costs of warehousing and delivery due to maintaining more than or less than the optimum inventory. This information, product by product and including purchased as well as manufactured items, is usually worked out in tabular or chart form for ready reference when making scheduling decisions.

The logistics of warehousing can be summed up as doing whatever is required in order to accomplish optimization of inventory. The result can be accepted as optimal only if cost and availability factors are both at the best possible level.

The use of electronic data processing has greatly increased the effectiveness of item-by-item inventory control of normal stocks. However there will always be a need for supplemental "old-style" controls, for example in very small warehouses operating under conditions of temporary surge or decrease in the "in-and-out" flow of a relatively few items. The small size and temporary nature of such a warehousing problem make costly machine accounting less necessary as well as too expensive when measured against the relatively small number of items.

The basic principle of the slide rule is that two scales of values, placed side by side, may be adjusted so that establishment of a point on one scale permits the measurement or determination of a value on the other scale. This device is useful in warehouse control. If the planned maximum inventory of 500 units of a particular item is on hand and 100 units are shipped to customers in the first week, the warehouse has a five-week supply at this rate of withdrawal. If in this same first week shipment of this item from the factory totals 25 units, the warehouse is on a twenty-week replacement of inventory basis for the item. Scales constructed to show a range of values may be placed side by side, and the effect of these different rates measured and evaluated. This example is simplified to the point of little usefulness in itself. When three or more variables are so scaled and interrelated that they point to the mathematically best relation between current use rate, stock on hand, and replacement of stock rate, usefulness of this type of charting can be significant. Like the engineer's slide rule, inventory control charts are easier to use than tables, or than solving mathematics equations.

Avoiding inventory surge problems

Rare indeed is the warehouse control system that is never confronted with a surge in inventory far in excess of normal capacity. From the point of view of logistics, it may be least costly to accept and deal with an inventory surge when it happens than to construct higher-capacity conveyors and larger storage spaces. This is because the surge may, predictably, occur for only a few days each year or for a few months during each business cycle of boom and depression. When it comes the surge may develop so rapidly as to turn the conveyor, operating at its normal rate, into a "choke point." Emergency handling must then be developed, preferably at a different location. For example, by means of temporary lease of storage space, excessive investment in space needed only for surge conditions can be avoided. For this discussion it is assumed that logistical calculation has shown that the surge is best met as an unplanned-for emergency situation.

Of great importance is avoidance of interference with the normal flow of merchandise. An example of such interference is filling both stacks or piles in a two-stack bay or area, then shipping to customers or to secondary warehouses direct from the production line. This violates the procedure of keeping quality at peak by shipping the oldest inventory first. Here the newest product is moving out, and the warehouse inventory is becoming older every day. Another example is piling an excess of product A on top of a part stack of product B. To get at B, all of product A has to be removed. Often the pile is completely turned over, and the problem may be repeated when it becomes necessary to ship some or all of product A. Finally the surge inventory, as it comes in may be placed in emergency piles in some of the aisles. This reduces the efficiency of the warehouse workers by forcing detours or by denying access to the oldest inventory of a particular product.

The surge problem is one of the reasons for the great increase in use of rented warehouse space. Public warehouses can absorb surge inventory in part because one product has its peak at a different time than another. Hence space devoted to surge inventory can be used to a greater extent. Public warehouses tend to have more space available since they must be prepared to take on new customers. The same location can sometimes be used for merchandise of like nature even though belonging to rival concerns, thus economizing in space usage. If the surge inventory problem is due to the requirements of particular customers, location of the public warehouses can be readily adjusted to these facts; this may facilitate obtaining customer cooperation by making it convenient for him to take in surge inventory as he can make room for it in his own plant. Thus public warehouses especially at the secondary locations can reduce the cost and facilitate handling of inventory surge situations.

Warehousing of packaged merchandise may be described as involving a logistical combination of well-selected locations, design for and accomplishment of efficient normal operation, a workable procedure for dealing with surges in inventory, and excellent paperwork procedures. The goal is optimum effectiveness and lowest possible unit cost. Though often overlooked or taken for granted, the quality of the paperwork procedures does influence both cost and customer relations. The intimacy of the interrelation between the paperwork and the rest of the warehouse factors is increasing because of self-identification of packages and the growing use of electronic data processing.

The ideal warehouse of the future may be visualized as being a kind of machine. At its heart will be the electronic data processing machines. Packages will identify themselves as they enter the building and will be directed to the proper location and there automatically piled or stacked. When a shipment is planned, the necessary instructions will be fed into the EDP. It will cause removal of the correct packages from the stacks and their movement on conveyors to the loading point where they will be assembled and hand loaded or machine loaded into the transportation equipment as required. While being loaded, the EDP will have adjusted the inventory, completed the shipping papers and informed the customer or the secondary warehouse of the shipment. Thus the paperwork, instead of lagging behind the inventory and shipment actions will be a part of and *to some extent* will control and direct the operation of the warehouse: *to some extent,* because skilled men will be needed to plan and program the instructions, to maintain the electronic and other machinery, and to cooperate in such actions as truck or freight car loading or unloading. EDP does not think for itself. It solves logistics problems only to the extent of the data and the instructions provided it. Human skill alone can prevent errors, just as at present.

Since about 1935 transportation has become a "buyer's market." There has been a dramatic increase in available user choices. The best equipment, best service and best "deal" must be sought out and found by each user. This transportation choice must be proved right by being coordinated carefully with warehouse problems and costs, inventory levels, production schedules and customer promises; also with packaging and securement of lading costs and annoyances versus alternative containerization possibilities and cost. Logistical cost reductions and service improvements don't just happen. They must be achieved for each commodity and each shipment.

Chapter VI

LOGISTICAL ASPECTS OF PRIVATE CARRIAGE

In recent years the increase in amount and relative importance of private carriage of freight has often been cited as a major cause of the plight of those common carriers that happen at the time to be in financial trouble. The exact figures are not known because much private carriage is unreported. Also some of the available statistics lump private and so-called exempt or unregulated for-hire carriage together. However, it is certain that private carriage of freight is an important competitor, particularly of regulated common carriers such as railroads and common carrier truck enterprises.

The Transportation Center at Northwestern University recently reported the initial findings of its Private Carriage Research Project. Important points from these findings are as follows:[1]

". . . approximately fifty-eight per cent of the nation's manufacturers made some use of private carriage in 1961, as compared with about fifty-two per cent in 1957.

"Firms which own or lease over-the-road vehicles haul about thirty-nine per cent of their own inter-city freight. . . ."[2]

Based on its Survey of Shippers, the Transportation Center found that the reporting manufacturers had increased their average fleet size to "13.8 trucks in 1961, as against 10.5

[1] As reported in National Defense Transportation Journal, article by Mark Reinsberg, January-February, 1963, Washington, D.C., pp. 37–39 and 50–53.
[2] Ibid., p. 38.

101

trucks in 1957—a growth of over 23 per cent."[3] Since the 1961 over-the-road trucks reported were probably more efficient and larger, the increase in importance of private carriage is emphasized by these data.

The Transportation Center Survey showed that some industries are much more likely to use private trucks than others. It follows that "the percentage of tonnage shipped in private vehicles varies widely from industry to industry." The Transportation Center stated that "we found . . . only one weighty consideration tending to move a firm toward proprietary trucking." This was that firms "with short-haul inter-city traffic, in a radius of 200–300 miles, use private trucking to a considerably greater extent than firms with long-haul traffic."[4]

The Transportation Center found that all "the more important results of our studies suggest that there are economies of scale in trucking operations. . . . Traffic and transportation costs (which make up about fifty per cent of total costs) decline with increases in output. . . . As a further corroboration . . . it was found that expanding firms tend to decrease their operating ratio. . . ."[5]

The Transportation Center attempted to analyze the relation between use of railroad freight and use of trucks. It found that

"In the distribution of total industry tonnage by mode, 1957–61 rail's share declined substantially. Both regulated and unregulated trucking gained, though omissions in data supplied the Center made it difficult to determine which of the two modes gained most proportionally. . . ."[6]

"The decisions of individual shippers, and the decisions of rate-makers, may not provide the explanations we are seeking. To ask how proprietary trucking fits into the nation-wide panorama, the growth and location trends of an industry, is to be reminded that private trucks and regu-

---

[3] *Ibid.*, p. 38.
[4] *Ibid.*, p. 38.
[5] *Ibid.*, p. 39.
[6] *Ibid.*, p. 51.

lated trucks are part of a single technology which is gaining in use relative to an older technology, the railroads.

"One of the great efficiency advantages of rail, it has always been thought, is derived from the long haul. Yet, we find that the average length of haul by truck is increasing: it is reaching out, according to our figures, into more and more distant markets. And the distance profile of trucking, rather than getting smaller because of decentralization of production, is actually stretching farther."[7]

The Transportation Center offered some so-labeled *diffident opinions,* as follows:

" . . . all forms of carriage—common, private, or exempt —are derived functions. Upset the established production patterns of an industry and you upset the balance of transportation serving that industry . . . we can be certain that transportation will reflect many kinds of industrial change with extreme sensitivity.

"In viewing the role of proprietary trucking within numbers of firms in each industry, the Center finds a complexity that cannot be eased by deploring the data or doubling the methodology. By its sheer pervasiveness in all sectors of the nation's economy, private carriage has emerged as the indicator of some widespread reality. At the very least, private carriage is part of a more intense, variable fabric of producer capacities and consumer expectations. It may also be evidence of an increasingly broad shift, throughout many categories of industry, from price to service competition. . . .

"We know very little as yet, about private carriage in multiplant operations, where transportation might serve to integrate production. . . . The whole matter of investment, reinvestment and disinvestment in trucking operations is virtually unresearched, and we have made only a beginning in studies of rate of return. We are continuing our research."[8]

---

[7] *Ibid.,* p. 51.
[8] *Ibid.,* p. 52.

Pioneer and modern American transportation compared

The Transportation Center Private Carriage Research Project is of great interest to the manufacturer or distributor or retailer who is considering undertaking some or all of his own transportation. This study, most comprehensive and basic to date, will assist him in his logistics calculation, that is, in deciding whether and how to engage in private carriage.

The Transportation Center offered as one of its so-called *diffident opinions,* the concept that "all forms of carriage—common, private or exempt—are derived functions." This brief statement raises one of the fundamental questions involving transportation, namely, its role in creating economic growth as measured by an increase in the GNP, the Gross National Product.

The Northwestern University statement may be paraphrased as a tentative conclusion that transportation is affected by changes in production patterns, rather than the reverse concept that changes in transportation cause the changes in production patterns. "Upset the established patterns of an industry and you upset the balance of transportation serving that industry . . . we can be certain that transportation will reflect many kinds of industrial change with extreme sensitivity . . . private carriage is part of a more intense variable fabric of producer capacities and consumer expectations. It may also be evidence of an increasingly broad shift . . . from price to service competition."[9]

This discussion reminds one of the dilemma as to which comes first, the chicken or the egg. The question is whether creation of form utility (i.e., manufacturing) precedes creation of time and location utilities (i.e., transportation). The Transportation Center's so-called *diffident opinion* is that the dominant factor is change in production and that "transportation will reflect many kinds of industrial change with extreme sensitivity."[10]

---

[9] *Ibid.,* p. 52.
[10] *Ibid.,* p. 52.

The first century of mechanized transportation, ending about 1910, seemed to prove the reverse of this diffident opinion. The railroads and the river and lake paddlewheel steamboats, as they penetrated the American continent, were said to have opened the West. That is, they seemed to have created the opportunity for colonists to produce agricultural, mineral and eventually manufactured products. Underdeveloped countries, or underdeveloped regions such as Northern Canada and Alaska, are said today to be in the same pioneer stage as was the American West during the Nineteenth Century. For such an underdeveloped area, creation of modern mechanized transportation facilities (i.e., time and location utilities) apparently precedes and makes possible production (i.e., form utility).

In modern America the choice is not between primitive private transportation on the backs of men or animals, or the pioneer railroad or steamboat. The choice is between several different modes of mechanized transportation, each further proliferated into numerous competing carriers and into for-hire and private carriage. Under this condition of multiple choice there is inevitable over-capacity of transportation, viewed as a whole. American transportation may be thought of as like a plastic when it is in its liquid form. It can then be made to flow into molds. Once in a mold it hardens into a new form or arrangement. In the same way, present-day transportation responds to changes in the location of production. In making this sort of adjustment it exhibits extreme sensitivity to changes in production patterns, such as the trend toward decentralization of industry, or the development of service competition.

Superior ability of transportation to *flow as a plastic* does, and thus acquire new form or shape, is one of the inherent advantages of private carriage. For-hire carriage is inevitably slower in its adjustment to new conditions, though it also does so eventually.

THE GRAY AREA IN TRUCKING AFFECTS PRIVATE CARRIAGE

An executive in charge of private carriage seeks to render the desired transportation service and at the same time reduce unit cost. This policy goal is an incentive to find and carry whatever legal and proper return-haul cargo can be obtained that does not interfere unduly with the desired service. Compared with common or contract carriage, an inherent disadvantage of private carriage is its inability to obtain the same proportion of back-haul as is obtained by the for-hire carrier. Of course there are exceptions, but most private carriage consists in a one-direction loaded movement with empty return haul in the other direction.

The Transportation Association of America in 1961 prepared an eight-page review of the illegal for-hire trucking problem.[11] The following excerpts describe the problem, particularly in relation to private carriage.

"The public and the economic welfare of our country depend on a healthy, well-balanced transportation system. Such a system—consisting of all forms of regulated for-hire carriers, plus bona fide exempt and private carriers—cannot remain dependable and serve the public efficiently if it is permitted to be weakened by unfair competition from illegally operated carriers.

"Today, shippers enjoy the benefits of a wide choice of carriers of several modes, both regulated and unregulated, and of stability of rates of regulated carriers. The latter rates, of course, tend to act as a ceiling since unregulated carriers can use published rates as their starting point when quoting lower rates. They also do not have to comply with strict service requirements applicable to regulated carriers. Regulated carriers, on the other hand, are in theory at least, authorized to operate in specific areas where for-hire transportation is to be handled exclusively by such carriers. Unfortunately, the line of demarkation between legal and

---

[11] Illegal For-hire Trucking Problem, prepared for the Committee Against Unauthorized Transportation, by the Transportation Association of America, Washington, D.C., July, 1961.

illegal for-hire transportation is not sufficiently clear to prevent some carriers from engaging in the marginal "gray area" of for-hire practices without operating authority from the ICC.

"Therefore, those that are being hurt are common and contract motor carriers, railroads, bona fide exempt for-hire haulers, and law-abiding shippers who refrain from illegal practices and thereby try to compete fairly, from the standpoint of transport costs, in the various markets across the country. Unfortunately, even the law-abiding exempt haulers and private carriers tend to get a black eye when some of those in their respective groups start transporting commodities illegally.

"In attempting to compete with the illegal truckers, railroads and authorized motor carriers must either maintain the current level of rates and risk substantial diversion of traffic or establish reduced rates. Yet the illegal operators can still quote spot rates and get the traffic. In a number of cases, however, the regulated carriers, suffering from increased unit costs from the loss of traffic, have been forced to increase their rates. This tends, of course, to encourage the additional diversion of traffic from the authorized carriers.

"Illegal operations, which create an adverse effect through the deterioration in the quantity and quality of authorized carriers' services needed to promote the nation's economy, tend to cause a reduction in the number of authorized carriers available, in the frequency of their schedule, and in the size of their fleets. Shippers and receivers using regulated carrier services are not only affected by this but also are adversely affected by unfair competition, having to compete with firms which move the same commodities in trucks that charge less than published rates. What is perhaps worse, these law-abiding shippers and carriers may feel obligated to engage in illegal practices to protect themselves against competitors who engage in such practices."[12]

---

[12] *Ibid.,* p. 3.

The dividing line between for-hire and private carriage

"There are a number of trucking operations probably being conducted today without the knowledge of the operator that they are illegal in nature. In all probability, however, the majority of these illegal operations are conducted with full knowledge that they are in violation of inter-state or intra-state regulations.

"Because of the competitive impact of unauthorized carriers on the regulated carrier industry, the ICC in a series of cases has clarified the distinction between a lawful private carrier and a for-hire carrier. The following are the types of arrangements used in inter-state trucking which are generally considered legal in nature:

"1. *A shipper transporting his own goods* in his own vehicle with his own driver in bona fide furtherance of his primary business, provided it is a non-carrier one.

"2. *Bona fide common and contract carriers and brokers* conducting operations with proper ICC and state authority.

"3. *A person transporting commodities specifically exempt* from regulation; i.e., agricultural products.

"4. *An owner-operator leasing for 30 days or more to a regulated carrier* and transporting goods under the carrier's authority.

"5. *Trip leasing by an exempt agricultural hauler to an authorized carrier for a return load to his point of origin.*

"6. *A shipper leasing a motor vehicle without driver from a bona fide leasing company* and using this vehicle to transport goods in the furtherance of his primary non-transport business."[13]

"Suggestions involving remedial action made at the National Conference on Illegal For-Hire Trucking show that there are a number of things that might be done to resolve the illegal trucking problem.

---

[13] *Ibid.,* p. 5.

"The following could be accomplished under present laws:

"(1) Increase cooperation among state and Federal agencies and authorized carriers.

"(2) Educate shippers concerning illegal practices.

"(3) Encourage both shippers and carriers being placed at a disadvantage by illegal for-hire transport practices to bring them to the attention of state and/or Federal regulatory officials.

"(4) Define more clearly who may transport goods for compensation, and also ICC regulations on motor vehicle leasing.

"(5) Permit the ICC to take court action against a carrier in any state in which it operates regardless of where it can be served and to join a shipper as a party defendant without regard to where the shippers may be served.

"(6) Increase ICC and state regulatory commissions' funds for enforcement."[14]

USER CHARGES AFFECT PRIVATE CARRIAGE

Encouragement and stimulus for individuals and business enterprises to use their own private transportation has come, in an important degree, from three inter-related factors:

1. Automobiles, trucks, barges, vessels, and airplanes when used for private purposes are unregulated except as to matters involving safety. Common carriers, on the other hand, being regulated must comply with necessary but cumbersome rules. Common carriers often are unable to make decisions and then act quickly. Frequently for-hire carriers continue to impose freight rate or service conditions on would-be users, even though the latter can reduce unit cost and improve service by turning to private carriage.

2. Construction of new high-capacity highways, also improved navigation channels and new and finer airports permits

---

[14] *Ibid.*, p. 7.

less costly and more efficient operation by all kinds of carriers, whether for-hire or private. For the would-be private carrier, such improvements make long-range estimates of unit operating cost both lower and more accurate. This reduces the risk-element in an executive's decision to undertake expenditures for entrance into private carriage by highway, by river or canal or by air.

3. To the extent that the new facilities recover in tolls or user charges less than their actual cost, the private operator of trucks or barges or airplanes has obtained a cost reduction that cannot be obtained by a carrier not using the facilities, such as a railroad or pipeline. This further encourages the use of private carriage. The following brief survey is, therefore, pertinent to the subject of private carriage.

Navigation user charges

The first lighthouse built within the present United States was at Boston in 1716, nearly 250 years ago. It was supported by a special toll, or user charge, levied by the town of Boston upon all vessels. In October 1789, Alexander Hamilton offered on behalf of the newly formed Federal Government to take over all lighthouses. Hamilton said the take-over was essential because the tonnage tax on shipping had become the Federal Government's taxation right, and could no longer be levied by a state or city. The Boston and other local user charges for lighthouses were then discontinued.

In 1845, Colonel Robert E. Lee of the Corps of Engineers suggested, and at federal expense constructed, diversion works that prevented the Mississippi River from adopting a new channel through what is now East St. Louis. Thus St. Louis avoided becoming a non-river city. This assistance from the Army Corps of Engineers was one of the first steps toward its present-day responsibility for river channel improvement and maintenance at general taxpayer expense, without direct collection from users of any portion of its cost by means of user charges.

The improved St. Lawrence Seaway was constructed

jointly by the United States and Canada. Both countries are collecting user charges from vessels using the channels and locks. On April 5, 1962, President Kennedy in his Message on Transportation asked the Congress to extend the principle of user charges to all of the inland waterways. He recommended a tax of 2 cents per gallon on all fuels used by towboats engaged in shallow-draft navigation.

Highway user charges

In 1924, Judge J. M. Lowe, in a volume entitled The National Old Trails Road, discussed the subject of national highways. He was speaking and writing in his role as president of an association bearing the same name:

> "We have fallen upon a time when the insignificant wagon roads of the country demand a place on the stage of progress. Where improved, they carry more passengers, daily, than the railroads and steamboats combined and, if not now, are destined in the near future, to carry the greater percentage of local freight traffic. . . . Strange as it may seem, there will be no rivaling conflict between these different methods of transportation—the one supplements and adds to the benefit of the other. No use now to raise the question as to which should have been first developed, but we started right when we began the construction of the Cumberland Road [from Cumberland, Maryland to the Ohio River at Wheeling] . . . in 1806, by the General Government. We had the correct idea, too, when we started to build trunk lines first, to be followed later by feeder roads, the common sense theory afterwards adopted by the railroads."[15]

The first Federal-Aid Road Act, passed by Congress in 1916, provided that roads constructed with federal funds were to be toll free. However the federal and local levies such as license and fuel taxes are, in fact, user charges. Present federal legislation specifically levies an extra fuel tax to be placed in a

---

[15] J. M. Lowe, National Old Trails Road Association, Kansas City, Missouri, 1924, pp. 9–10.

Highway Trust Fund and used to pay for the new 41,000-mile system of super highways.

Aviation user charges

The history of commmercial airport financing is one of municipal responsibility aided by generous grants from the federal government. The local government must carry the resulting debt service (interest and repayment of the principal sum) and also maintain the airport. This need for income has resulted in the charging of landing fees as well as airport building rental charges. These landing fees are user charges.

On April 5, 1962, a Presidential Message on transportation was sent to Congress. In this important message the President made specific recommendations with respect to user charges, as follows:

"Aviation. For commercial airlines, I have suggested (a) continuation of the 2-cents-per-gallon net tax on gasoline and extension of the tax rate to all jet fuels; and (b) a 5% tax on airline tickets. . . . For general aviation . . . a fuel tax of 3 cents per gallon is recommended."

PHYSICAL DISTRIBUTION FACILITATED BY PRIVATE CARRIAGE

It is frequently true that the lowest carrier charge for transportation is not the one that, in combination with everything else, produces the lowest unit cost and most desirable service for the entire movement. In fact, in some cases use of a fast and expensive private or for-hire airplane will yield the lowest over-all cost to the shipper because of related savings due to the time factor. Much of Canada and Alaska are being successfully opened up as a new and vast frontier by the cargo-airplane. It overcomes its inherent cost handicap by combining speed with a high degree of reliability. When choosing transportation one cannot assume that today's slow railroad switching service, or today's awkward and slow procession of loaded and empty private or for-hire trucks is the best or proper way. There must be better ways, and they must be found and used.

Air freight as an example of the physical distribution concept

As the pioneer study of air freight stated, "Air freight . . . is faster than previous methods. . . . The actual rate of speed in transportation is not the only factor involved in a businessman's appraisal of speed. Most frequently he is more interested in total elapsed time. . . . Thus speed . . . includes efficiency in using fast transportation facilities and other considerations, such as the amount of handling and trans-shipments involved.[16]

"Similarly with cost. . . . Ton-mile cost figures . . . are a reflection of a number of variables in addition to price, including distance, size of shipment, type of commodity, and type of service . . . air freight is known . . . as premium transportation, an accurate term if it is used to mean that you pay more and get more.[17]

"The above observations on speed and cost clearly show that . . . it is necessary to take a look at the transportation package, at what a business really buys at any given cost when it is moving things from one place to another.[18]

"In addition to speed, the transportation package includes such items as the following:

1) Reliability
2) Availability of service
3) Management
4) Design characteristics of equipment
5) Effect on other costs
    a) inventory
    b) warehousing
    c) packaging and packing
    d) handling[19]

---

[16] The Role of Air Freight in Physical Distribution, H. T. Lewis, J. W. Culliton, J. D. Steele, Graduate School of Business Administration, Harvard University, Boston, Massachusetts, 1956, p. 8.

[17] *Ibid.*, pp. 8–9.

[18] *Ibid.*, p. 9.

[19] *Ibid.*, pp. 9–10.

"It will be seen throughout this report that reliability—that is, regular delivery according to established schedules—is frequently more important to business than speed. . . . Reliability has been, historically, an important factor in determining the place a new form of transportation will achieve in the total picture.[20]

"Management, as used here, refers to the management policies and practices of the companies furnishing the transportation. Two aspects are of especial significance. The first has to do with the technical operation of the transportation facilities, the establishment and maintenance of schedules, the maintenance and purchase of new and better equipment, and the maximum effectiveness with which the inherent advantages of a particular kind of transportation are used. The second has to do with services to the customer, the care with which shipments are followed through, and the attention given to emergencies.[21]

"Design characteristics of the equipment are more closely related to the nature of each type of transportation and have a large bearing upon the ultimate importance of any form of transportation.[22]

"Effect on other costs. On the frontispiece of this study is the following 1844 quotation from Dupuit: 'The ultimate purpose of a means of transportation ought not to be to reduce the expenses of transportation, but to reduce the expense of production.' The quotation aptly sums up the significance of the point being made here, with one notable exception. With distribution taking more than half the consumer's dollar, the ultimate purpose of transportation should be to reduce the expenses of production and distribution. The point is so extremely vital to the whole subject of this study that comment here would be superficial.[23]

"One proposal resulting from the research is that manage-

---

[20] *Ibid.,* p. 10.
[21] *Ibid.,* pp. 11, 12.
[22] *Ibid.,* p. 12.
[23] *Ibid.,* p. 13.

ment begin to examine physical distribution costs as one total package in order to get into better perspective the relationships between physical distribution and the rest of the business. . . . There is a great need for a re-thinking of the place of transportation in business operations.[24]

" . . . the fundamental requirement of any worthwhile analysis is an understanding of the traffic function as an integral part of procurement and distribution.[25]

"The purpose of the study was to analyze some of the effects the use of air freight might have upon the cost of physical distribution. Physical distribution was defined as including those activities that are involved in physically handling a product from the time it leaves finished goods inventory at the factory warehouse until it is drawn from inventory at a regional warehouse."[26]

"Storming," an example of ineffective physical distribution

In many factories there is a tendency to ship more than half of the month's quota of outbound finished products in the second half of the month. Often there is greatest concentration in the last week or even in the last few days of each month. The effect upon the shipping problem is to cause a month-end flurry of demand for empty freight cars, private and for-hire trucks, and barges. Need to arrange and pay for overtime also develops, since the workers who normally package and load outbound shipments will have a surge of work. Their surge will be concentrated even closer to the end of the month than that of the production workers.

The reason for this surge or drive to achieve the shipment quota may be related to the desire to schedule production runs that optimize unit production costs by reducing "down time" of machines. At the start of each month this scheduling policy is naturally dominant. As a result production of some orders is delayed. Others are produced even though they must then

[24] *Ibid.,* p. 106.
[25] *Ibid.,* p. 115.
[26] *Ibid.,* p. 119.

be placed in the warehouse until something else is made. This happens because the customer has ordered several different things, all to be assembled in one freight car or truck or barge.

Toward the end of each month the scheduling emphasis changes. Production is then planned even in small and costly lots, so as to complete orders and get them shipped. Everyone suddenly realizes that the actual rate of production during the relatively calm first half of the month was less than half of the month's production quota. Hence there must be scheduled in addition to the "fill-out orders," other production runs that will overcome the deficit of the first half of the month. Thus with a burst of energy, workers, machines and management meet their goals.

The effect of this kind of poor, but often unavoidable variation in the nature and quantity of orders released to the plant by the production-scheduling staff has been described, in extreme form, as it exists in Russian industry. As David Granick points out

"Production-scheduling is a favorite subject for self-castigation in Russian industrial management circles. Scheduling of materials into the factory, of the work through the various shops, and of the finished product out onto the railroad freight cars is notoriously poor. As a result, Soviet industry is highly subject to a practice which the Russians fittingly call 'storming'."[27]

"In American industry, this practice finds its expression in uneven shipments of finished goods out of the plant. . . . In Russian industry, on the other hand, the greater autonomy of each individual shop makes its influence felt. . . . Thus the problem of 'storming' in the Soviet Union is not just that of piling up of shipments out of the factory, but also of the piling up of shipments from one shop to the next in the production cycle."[28]

---

[27] The Red Executive, A Study of the Organization Man in Russian Industry. David Granick, Anchor Books, Doubleday & Co., Garden City, New York, 1961, pp. 230–31.

[28] *Ibid.*, p. 233.

In both the air freight and the production-scheduling examples the conclusion emerges that physical distribution involves many factors in addition to transportation. Clearly, also, private carriage can supply more flexible and better service. Even at higher unit cost for the transportation itself, private carriage often permits achievement of lowest over-all cost as well as better service.

Discrimination, in its broadest sense, is the identification of differences, such as by tasting different flavors of ice cream. As used in transportation "undue" or "unjust" or "unfair" are used as adjectives or implied. The "gray area" and "user charges" are becoming more important questions because many believe the present situation is unduly discriminatory against common carriers, and therefore undesirably favorable to private carriage. Imposition of new or additional user charges, coupled with more accurate identification of the boundary between private carriage and for-hire carriage, is urged as a means of lessening discrimination. However, the new or additional user charges must not take from the user all of the benefit, even though thereby being insufficient to recover all the properly allocated costs.

Chapter VII

THE LOGISTICS OF FREIGHT RATES

In the United States the role of the common carrier as the dominant force in determining transportation prices has been accepted by the business community for at least a century. Beginning with the second quarter of the Nineteenth Century when the railroads became the principal supplier of land transportation, the general level of transportation prices has been largely established by them. As time went on, common carriers emerged also on the ocean, on coastal and inland waterways, on highways, in the air, and underground as pipelines. The past success of these rapidly growing and varied common carriers in proper pricing of their intangible product—transportation service—was attested to not only in transportation profits, but also in the high percentage of total traffic moved by common carriers.

Gradually "common law" concepts began to become regulatory legislation, at first administered by the courts. Today such laws apply to all common carriage and to much of contract carriage. For example, strict penalties are prescribed for failure to collect the exact amount of freight and passenger charges, which must be openly published for all to see. Neither more nor less can lawfully be collected.

The concept of a "zone of reasonableness" soon developed. This is a zone or range between rates unfairly high on one side and unfairly low on the other. Within this zone actual freight rates are permitted to be determined by the interplay of competitive forces. Millions of commodity rates have been made by American common carriers within this zone, usually resulting from "face-to-face" negotiations between a shipper and one or more carriers.

During this same early period, economists and political scientists were evolving their philosophy of common carriage, particularly in regard to railroads. Common carrier railroads were characterized by them as monopolies, natural, statutory or de facto, at least in part for the reason that sometimes a particular railroad was the only modern means of transportation available in some geographical area. This theoretical concept has been supported by two occasional kinds of happenings or evidence.

If the monopolistic leverage was strong enough the railroad by its actions and the results therefrom proved itself able to kill off some or all of its rival competition. As common carrier railroads grew in size they also became competitive with each other at certain points. Scholars came to believe that they then needed to be restrained from suicidal freight rate reducing tactics. Use of laws and regulatory decisions to provide this restraint was urged as better than to permit use of cartel devices. Development of private carriage and of strong but not suicidal inter-modal carrier competition has, in recent decades, raised doubts as to the assumption that the railroads and the other types of common carriers are inherently monopolistic.

Freight rates in the United States were initially considered to be largely in the nature of tolls. In fact, the word toll was commonly used by early railroads, particularly those which permitted use of their track by anyone possessed of flange-wheel wagons and supplying their own horses. Using this as a basis, it is possible to distinguish two of the major subdivisions within a freight rate. One part is the compensation or toll for the right to use the private route and its track. The other is a charge for the transportation service performed.

The toll approach to charging for the "fixed facilities" part of each passenger ticket or freight bill has not disappeared. Toll bridges, port wharfage charges and airport landing fees are all charges for the privilege of use that are related to the use but not to the relative usefulness of the particular passage or landing. So also in a broad sense is the payment by individuals and corporations of taxes levied to pay for navigation improvements, for air traffic control, or for city streets. The toll aspect is still used very little as a common carrier pricing factor. This is fortunate because freight charges, if consisting primarily of the toll factor, would then lack direct relation to the value of the particular transportation service to the particular shipper.

Freight rates are transportation prices

Common and contract carrier freight rates are market prices because:

1. They represent the price the carrier is willing to charge. In many cases he has become convinced that he cannot charge more without losing the traffic to a competitor or to private carriage.

2. They represent the price the shipper and receiver, either or both, are willing to pay. They would not make shipments at this price if they did not believe it to be fair and unlikely to be lowered without losing some necessary service element such as speed, freedom from damage or availability of equipment. In other words the service is worth this price to the shipper and receiver.

3. Freight rates are arrived at within the so-called zone of reasonableness by a negotiation or "dickering" process by the two parties, carrier and user.

4. After negotiations have been completed, the resulting freight rates are published in tariff form. Thus they become available to any shipper or receiver of the identified commodities between the identified points. They become the accepted market price.

5. They can be renegotiated and changed if circumstances and conditions change.

6. They can be withdrawn by the carrier, under certain conditions imposed by regulation.

7. They can be nullified by the shipper or receiver by refusal to ship at the rates.

COMMON CARRIERS NO LONGER DOMINATE

During the years since World War I, the philosophical concept of railroad and other common carriers as monopolies, natural or statutory or de facto, has been shattered by the fact of competition within every mode of transport and also competition between modes and with private carriage. Both regulated and unregulated carriers, whether common or contract in form, have shown surprising ability to compete. Clearly the notion that carrier competition must necessarily lead to mutually destructive freight rate wars is somewhat, if not completely, at variance with actual facts. Of course the present-day regulatory environment is an important foundation factor. Indeed, regulation must be given credit for forestalling incipient rate wars by dealing effectively with the sources of conflict.

This new competitive situation is rearranging transportation. Everywhere in the United States a declining percentage of the total traffic is available to and is being obtained by the common carriers. An increasing percentage of freight transportation is being performed by contract carriers and by owners for their own account and in privately operated equipment. These changes have lessened the universality of common carrier freight rates, thus reducing their former leverage power to determine the going rate or market price at which actual transportation is performed.

Highway competition has become universal

Competition of the ubiquitous motor truck is present at every local railroad station, at every river landing, and at every airport. There is scarcely a single commodity or bulk material that can truly be considered completely captive to any one carrier or mode of transportation. Freight rate competition has become universal—between carriers and modes—due chiefly to the development of the paved rural highway and the motor truck. Prior to World War I there were few motor trucks. Now they are everywhere, go everywhere, carry everything. Between World War I and II, there was an increasing invasion by the motor truck of intercity and even of transcontinental transportation, and private truck transportation became commonplace. Trucks supplement every other mode of transportation by handling shipments to and from terminals and transfer points. Even this supplemental role is competitive in character since it takes the place of some other mode or means.

Historians who observe present-day facts against the backdrop of past centuries see today and tomorrow as evolving out of our yesterdays. Observing transportation from this broad historical perspective, the use of rural paths and roads for transportation is seen to have been supplemental to the easier and more efficient water transportation. This supplemental pre-railroad role continued, with only one brief exception, until invention of higher-powered highway vehicles than those drawn by horses. This exception, of importance only to historians, was the relatively short period of time before and after 1800, of improved gravel turnpike roads used chiefly by stagecoaches. By 1850, the rural road again had lapsed into disuse for long-distance transport. It had again become non-competitive and purely supplemental, this time to the common carrier railroad. This was the situation in the United States before about 1924.

Today highway and truck evolution has made private transportation of one's own freight easy and relatively inexpensive. Any individual can own or rent a truck. Any business enterprise can supply its own private transportation to whatever extent and for whatever distance it desires. This fact of ease of entry upon performance of one's own transportation provides a new kind of pressure upon freight rates. For example, because it can come into existence anywhere, private truck transportation cost is becoming the competitive upper limit of the common-carrier freight rate zone of reasonableness.

Private carriage is causing discard of "ability to pay" as a rate-making factor

An important change in the fundamentals of freight rate-making that is modifying governmental concepts and regulatory decisions, is with respect to the relative emphasis on each of the transportation characteristics. Privately owned transportation is forcing downward the whole upper range of freight rates, to the extent that it was originally designed in terms of "ability to pay." The upper limit is becoming private carriage operating cost. Another change caused by motor trucks is in the extent of packaging, securement and protection needed, both in terms of materials and in terms of cost. The motor truck usually requires far less materials, labor and cost for these necessary operations, and its competition must adjust to these facts.

As already pointed out, the concept of the zone of reasonableness, or range within which freight rates are actually negotiated, is being changed by the motor truck. This zone has been considered to be the range of possible rates between out-of-pocket cost of the particular carrier and the decision of a regulatory agency as to the maximum beyond which rates would be considered to be unfairly high. The zone of reasonableness concept is shifting toward both minimum and maximum determinations based on the cost facts of the most favorably situated carriers by any modes that are actually competing at the moment for the particular traffic. The actual rate selected within such a zone is related to cost, not to "ability to pay."

Former attitudes as to the importance of preserving rate relations also are changing. For example, railroad common carriers have, in recent years, become increasingly reluctant to widen the application of "water-compelled" and "truck-compelled" rates beyond the scope of the actual competition. Thus the maintenance of geographical and commercial relationships achieved through years of rail freight rate adjustment based on the "value of service" concept is not any longer considered an ironclad requirement.

Great Britain has deregulated

At this point, it is appropriate to review how Great Britain in recent years has changed its concepts as to proper railroad freight rates, particularly since the British railroads were nationalized in 1947.

Even though British railroads are nationalized, most of the trucks are not. Common and contract trucks can and do compete against nationalized modes of transport. Most important as a British competition factor is private carriage, which continues its rapid growth.

In 1937, the British Parliament, in its Road and Rail Traffic Act of that year, had permitted railroad common carriers to make transportation contracts at negotiated rates under rules that provided for some degree of publicity and for review of appeals made on grounds of discrimination between shippers. The 1953 Transportation Act went a step further by permitting the nationalized British Railways to make contracts secretly when it considered it necessary to do so in order to meet actual competitive conditions.

Clearly, therefore, the British Government has recently changed two important public policies. First, Parliament has turned over to its nationalized railroad the power to make its own freight rates as it chooses. Presumably because private truck competition is unrestrained, Parliament has also freed competitive rail freight rates from all restraint. Second, rates made for movement by railroad could be in any suitable form, common or contract, published or secret, as decided or desired by the British railroad managers.

The extreme step taken by Great Britain of abandonment of anti-discrimination legislation destroys much of the value of freight rate regulation from the shipper standpoint. It does this by permitting self-determination by the managers of the nationalized carrier without other regulatory review, and especially by abandoning the traditional and important policy of open tariff publication. This return to secrecy as between shippers concerning the price each is paying to the same carrier may be practicable in Great Britain; it would be very undesirable in the United States. Such secret rate-making would lessen, and might even destroy, shipper confidence in the fairness of their transportation charges compared with those paid by their competitors. Even more important, it would deprive all the competing carriers and shippers of knowledge of the going or current freight rates on manufactured products.

NEW TYPES OF COMMON CARRIER FREIGHT RATES

United States common carriers are moving into a new era of transportation rate-making. Incentive rates, volume rates, "whole train" rates, contractually agreed rates—these are the innovation-type ideas being discussed and examined by carrier managements and by shippers and regulatory agencies today.

Incentive rates

In recent years it has become increasingly clear that the public was demanding both better service and lower transportation costs from common carriers. For example, beginning about 1949 railroads began to adjust their freight rates to meet their competition, and to try out new service ideas and new rate concepts. Of great importance are the new incentive-type freight rates designed to increase the efficiency of railroad operation. In developing such rates, railroads followed both truck and barge rate practices, also their own experience.

The theory behind the incentive type of freight rate is to reduce cost by obtaining greater utilization of the capacity of the vehicle or barge. The incentive consists in offering a reduction in freight rate for the actual weight of the extra lading that exceeds the normal minimum weight. An example is a rate of $10 per ton, minimum weight 20 tons, and an alternating rate of $8 per ton, minimum weight 40 tons. The charge for the incentive increment of 20 tons is only $120 or at the reduced rate of $6 per ton. It may be published either as $8 per ton on the entire 40 tons, or as $6 per ton on the amount shipped in excess of 20 tons.

Volume rates

The second new approach in freight rates is the *volume rate*. Strange as it may seem today, volume rates offered by the railroads before the turn of the century were one of the causes leading to the enactment of the Interstate Commerce Act in 1887. One of the cases decided by the Interstate Commerce Commission in that first year condemned the practice of offering volume rates as opposed to public policy. In another early case in 1890, the Commission, in considering rates that the railroads attempted to justify on the basis of a quantity discount, said quite clearly that it was disapproving the rates because a concession to the large shipper as against the small was a doctrine at war with one of the basic purposes of the Interstate Commerce Act—to protect the small, weak user against larger and stronger shippers.

The volume rate is one that covers several carloads or truckloads or barge-loads shipped at one time, by one shipper, to one consignee, to one destination, and on one bill of lading. In 1939, the Interstate Commerce Commission gave its first approval to a railroad multiple car rate, on molasses from New Orleans to Peoria, Illinois. In this historic case the Commission departed from its prior decisions and found that the materially changed economic, industrial, and transportation conditions of today should be recognized. The Interstate Commerce Commission said that the molasses had been moving in barge-loads by water, and that therefore the advantage to the large shipper of lower cost volume transportation already existed. It followed that the situation would not be changed by the railroads seeking to obtain a larger share of the traffic by means of volume rates of their own. Typical American volume freight rates are for movements ranging from 500 to 3,500 tons offered by one shipper for movement to one consignee. These tonnages are not large enough to constitute an efficient American freight train load or barge tow. However, in movement of coal an annual volume has come into use. For example, for all coal moved in a calendar year in excess of 2,000,000 tons to a designated public utility plant, a rate reduction of 30 per cent may be offered. If the total movement is 3,000,000 tons, the over-all rate reduction would be 10 per cent.

French experience with "whole train" rates

The French National Railways have established freight rates for the movement of complete trainloads from point to point, which may be a prototype for similar trainload rates in the Common Market and, perhaps, in the United States.[1]

---

[1] These rates, designated as tariff numbers 103 and 104, are explained in Rene Bourgeois, *L'exploitation Commerciales des Chemins de Fer Francais,* Paris, 1960.

Certain conditions must be met before applying the French "whole train" tariff, as follows:

1. All cars in the train must move from the same origin to the same destination.
2. Shipper and consignee must be equipped with sufficient yard room to permit the dispatching or the receipt of complete trainloads.
3. The railroad only furnishes the line-haul and the road crew. The shipper makes up the train.
4. The train must consist of a minimum tonnage, but also must not exceed the maximum tonnage possible considering the power used and the grades.
5. Rates are available for all commodities. However, the trainload rates are usually used only for high-density bulk commodities such as coal, ore and petroleum products. Over one-fourth of total tonnage uses these rates.

Determination of the French "whole train" freight rates is by computing and subtracting discounts from the normal rates, as follows:

1. The carload commodity rate is reduced by a fixed amount. This fixed reduction increases as the tonnage of the train increases. This induces building up the train to its maximum allowable tonnage.
2. An additional incentive reduction is afforded if the shipper provides and uses his own cars, varying according to the carrying capacity of the cars.
3. Still another reduction is offered for regularity of use. The maximum reduction is given if the shipper loads a train on every normal working day for an entire month.
4. The total reduction under the normal single carload rates ranges from 39 per cent to 55 per cent.

Views on contract or agreed rates

Dr. G. Lloyd Wilson, in his book on New Departures in Freight Rate Making, defined contract or agreed rates as follows:

"In substance, this method of rate making consists of the establishment of a single rate per unit of shipment (hundred pounds or ton) for all shipments, sometimes without regard to the commodity or distance, in connection with all or a specified portion of the shipper's freight traffic for the period of time in which the contract is in effect. The contracts or agreements are usually conditioned upon the shipment of all or a specified portion of the shipper's traffic via the services of the contracting carrier. The agreements are . . . subject to public notice and the approval of the government transportation regulatory body having jurisdiction."[2]

After reviewing the tariff simplification and rate reduction advantages and the potentially undesirable effect, from the user point of view, of limiting or even eliminating freedom of choice, Dr. Wilson concluded that

"Whatever may be the merits or demerits of agreed freight rate arrangements, they should be open covenants, openly negotiated, and publicly approved."[3]

This point of view is in accord with Canadian procedures, and with American regulatory policies. It is in sharp contrast with British secrecy of contract negotiation between individual shippers and the nationalized British Railways Administration already discussed. In Great Britain, it is frankly urged that secrecy in determining contract rates is necessary. This is because it permits unlimited discrimination in pricing between customers, for example by reducing freight charges of a loyal customer and increasing freight charges of a customer who uses the railroad only as a "standby" service when his private trucks are for any reason unavailable.

Dr. Wilson listed fifteen factors that, to him, were significant in determining the reasonableness and relative fairness of Canadian-type agreed charges:

"1. All appropriate elements of cost.
2. All relevant factors of the charges of other carriers.

---

[2] G. Lloyd Wilson, New Departures in Freight Rate Making, Simmons-Boardman, New York, 1948, p. 25.
[3] Ibid., p. 30.

3. The savings to carriers. . . .

4. The relative costs to shippers . . . by different instrumentalities of transportation, as items in the total cost of handling freight [i.e., the logistical computation of alternatives].

5. The observance of out-of-pocket costs of the carriers as minima. . . .

6. The reasonable, competitive interest of the other carriers. . . .

7. The establishment and maintenance of . . . reasonable rate relationships between shippers, points or areas of production, markets, and commodities.

8. The consideration of the competitive interests of other shippers and consignees who use the same and other carrier's services. . . .

9. The adjustment of rates and charges . . . to adjust freight rates to changing price levels, costs and economic conditions. . . .

10. The availability of equitable rates upon the same or related bases to all who can demonstrate that they are entitled to them.

11. The establishment of rates after public hearing. . . .

12. The establishment of rates subject to the critical review of a government regulatory body. . . .

13. The establishment of freight rates upon bases which give proper but not undue consideration to the quantities shipped. . . .

14. The establishment of proper relationships between carload and less-than-carload rates so that each type of service defrays its proper share of costs. . . .

15. The preservation of the rights of shippers and carriers to have the lawfulness of the rates considered . . . [by] the Interstate Commerce Commission or by litigation in the courts."[4]

---

4 *Ibid.*, pp. 138–39.

EFFECT OF REGULATION ON COMMON CARRIER
FREIGHT RATES

American common carrier freight rates have been negotiated since 1887 against a background of impartial and judicial Interstate Commerce Commission regulation. This government agency has established broad rules to govern the rate-making procedure. These rules are based on concepts of fairness, negotiation within the zone of reasonableness and, above all, pitiless publicity of every freight rate action by any common carrier.

Negotiation of freight rates has been formalized in so far as procedure and precedents are concerned. The formal rules are partly derived from experience, and are partly prescribed by law and by the Interstate Commerce Commission. Precedents have defined and delimited the rights of carriers to price their transportation services. The goal of all concerned is to bring about establishment of openly published freight rates that will attract traffic to the particular common carrier.

The role of rate conferences

Economists devote much attention, in their theoretical studies, to the actions of rate conferences or bureaus. Their concern is with the actual or potential use of such agencies for collusive group decisions. They theorize that rate bureaus, if left unregulated, could acquire and use monopoly power either to drive a rival kind of transportation out of existence or to build a combine consisting of two or more rate bureaus acting together. In either case, the rate bureau or bureaus might then seek to administer freight rates so as to obtain excessively high gross revenues for their carrier members. Such gross revenues could become high net earnings or could result in keeping additional unneeded transportation capacity in existence. In either case, the freight rates would tend to lose all relation to cost of transportation. Users also consider regulation of bureau actions a necessity, though for more practical reasons.

The appeal procedure

There is an appeal procedure with many steps. It usually begins with an oral or written suggestion by a shipper that a commodity freight rate be established or be further reduced. Almost always this suggestion involves a rate reduction below the alternative level of so-called class rates. Sometimes the carrier makes the first suggestion. Carrier use of rate-making to develop and attract traffic is by no means dead.

Following the initial request by carrier or shipper are a series of actions involving committees of carriers. These steps include standing rate committee reports, hearings, and interim decisions by the carrier committees. Frequently there are several levels of carrier committees with provision for appeal from one level to the next higher group. The operation of these carrier committees is governed by rules filed with the Interstate Commerce Commission—rules designed to bring about publicity of all actions and facts. These rules likewise are designed to permit and encourage independent notice of individual action by any carrier. The rules are subject to approval and supervision, including modification when so decided, by the Interstate Commerce Commission.

Beyond these carrier actions and decisions are the state regulatory agencies, the Interstate Commerce Commission and the courts, constituting another series of appeal and decision steps. State and Federal officials and employees examine every commodity rate change during the 30 or more days that must elapse between filing date and effective date. Some rates are suspended before the effective date has been reached. Suspension is upon the government's own motion or is to permit further study of a complaint filed by another carrier or by a shipper. After hearing the suspended rates are affirmed, ordered modified, or ordered withdrawn.

This lengthy appeal chain may seem cumbersome and awkward. Actually, it is very necessary. It permits commodity rates to be negotiated to a conclusion after all appropriate facts have been obtained. It permits a shipper to keep his request alive and before the carriers in spite of opposition. It forces carriers to view requests impartially since unfair decisions are reversed or revised by government at some higher appeal level.

In contrast to this market-place type of rate-making, the suggestion has often been made that the Interstate Commerce Commission should determine *all* freight rates itself, thus eliminating the carrier procedural steps. This would throw an enormous additional burden onto the Interstate Commerce Commission.

Variety of concepts regarding cost

The economist does not use the term "cost" in the same way as do accountants, tax authorities, regulatory commissions, commerce attorneys, or traffic managers. Each of them tend to have a slightly different idea of the meaning of "cost." Hence it is easy to misinterpret modifying adjectives. For example, the term "marginal cost" does not imply to the economist (who is theorizing about perfect competition) either a loss or a deficit. Under conditions of theoretically perfect competition, it means to him that the price buyers are willing to pay and the cost that suppliers are willing to incur are the same. Clearly, it assumes recovery of total average cost. It identifies the point at which the average price obtained by a carrier is just large enough to cause him to maintain the desired transportation service. The revenue must cover both the direct and indirect costs, including payment of taxes, payment to owners, and payment of the cost of keeping the enterprise in healthy existence by maintenance and replacement. Confusion may result because to noneconomists the word "marginal" seems to be equivalent to minimum or "out-of-pocket." Actually both because it is an average, and because it is derived from conditions of perfect competition, marginal cost or price has little application to the realities of transportation.

Economic cost is another vague term, hard to apply to reality. An example is a railroad tunnel. The railroad company accountant would naturally report actual outlays for tunnel maintenance, for interest on its cost and for annual amortization of this investment. However, the latter two expenses are not considered by some economists to be economic cost. The economist would classify them as expenses being incurred on account of "sunk capital," that is, capital that can never be recovered. If the railroad is discontinued, the tunnel becomes a worthless hole in the ground. This is an example where economic cost might be considered to be something less than accounting cost. An opposite example is of a street railway enterprise that has abandoned its car lines and substituted busses. In its own accounts, it gets rid of the cost of maintaining its track including the cost of paving between the rails. An impartial survey, it may be further assumed, has shown that the bus company, through fuel and other taxes, is not making full payment toward the maintenance and traffic control of the city streets that it uses. Its economic cost should be its bus operating expenses, plus taxes and other overhead charges, including profit, and also a proper additional charge for street maintenance. In this instance the economic cost would be considered to be something greater than the accounting cost.

Three other cost terms are used somewhat loosely, especially by those interested in negotiating freight rates:

a. By out-of-pocket cost is meant the short-run variable costs that accountants can assign or apportion directly, and with a high degree of accuracy in allocation, to a particular transportation service performed between two points.

b. By incremental cost is meant out-of-pocket cost plus an additional estimated amount that covers other costs, specifically the long-run variable cost that can also be assigned and apportioned with a high degree of accuracy. Incremental cost may be defined as the increase in total costs caused by and resulting from a specific expansion in volume of business.

c. Fully distributed cost includes out-of-pocket or incremental cost plus an estimated amount to cover average overhead costs. This average, if used to compute all freight rates, would recover full average cost from each shipment.[5]

---

[5] W. J. Baumol and others, The Role of Cost in the Minimum Pricing of Railroad Services, Journal of Business, Vol. XXXV, No. 4, October 1962, University of Chicago, p. 2.

Out-of-pocket cost, incremental cost, and fully distributed cost are not the same as, and should not be confused with, minimum and maximum, which are regulatory standards and have their own relation to costs.

Use of cost in rate negotiations

There are three cost elements in every freight rate. These are the terminal, road-haul and overhead costs. The terminal and road-haul costs, taken together, may be compared with out-of-pocket or incremental costs as defined above. This comparison is valid only if the build-up is the same. Thus to a user, terminal cost includes securement of lading and use of his company's tractor to haul the loaded trailer or container to the railroad yard or truck terminal, if such extra costs are required. The railroad or trucker might disregard these costs when computing his out-of-pocket expense.

Other factors in negotiating freight rates based at least in part on cost include the amount of "taper" as distance increases. This depends on the relation between one-time terminal costs and road-haul costs that are about the same for each mile. Use of the normally unused extra capacity of the vehicle, for example, by a second or third tier of cartons adds to loading cost and reduces carrier cost. Regularity of volume offered for shipment also reduces carrier cost, especially if the result is to fill out existing freight trains. The shipper point of view is that every rail- or road-mile is the same as every other mile; the cost-minded carrier will surely survey his actual situation. Heavy grades and very little return-haul tonnage to be solicited and obtained can result in abnormally high actual costs.

OBSTACLES TO EFFECTIVE USE OF ELECTRONIC DATA PROCESSING IN SHIPPER-CARRIER TRANSACTIONS

Charles Duffy in a recent speech has ably summarized the problem of use of electronic data processing as a key procedural tool for the logistical control of freight rates by shippers and carriers. Excerpts from his speech follow:[6]

---

[6] C. D. Duffy, Delta Nu Alpha Transportation Fraternity, Pittsburgh Chapter, March 1962. Mimeographed excerpts from report of speech.

The size of the clerical problem

"In round figures, the best authorities estimate that the
I.C.C. has 43 trillion rates on file in their tariff files that occupy
5,366 linear feet—over a mile—of filing space. Each year the
I.C.C. receives 800,000 new pages of tariff material (at an estimated publication cost of $12 per page, or a gross cost of $9,-
600,000) in 188,000 separate publications.

"Similar authorities estimate, and they are rough estimates:

Two billion shipments are made in the United States
each year.

At least one billion shipments are other than parcel post,
which are hereafter ignored.

Only 30,000,000 are carload shipments.

There are 96,000 origins and destinations.

There are 10,000 basic commodities listed in both the
rail and truck classifications, plus many thousands of
commodity descriptions for individual commodity rates.

There are 17,000 common carrier trucklines in the
United States.

$1.00 per shipment is the direct paperwork cost of a
small truck shipment to a truckline.

40 to 50 cents is the freight bill processing cost to an
industrial shipper (ignoring routing and preliminary
related documentation like invoicing, labeling, shipping
notices, etc.).

Rail clerical costs are approximately $10.00 per car,
and LCL paperwork costs $2.50 per shipment.

"1. Broadly, each shipper and carrier is increasingly
streamlining his paperwork internally to (a) speed
transactions, (b) reduce costs, and (c) obtain more
meaningful information for management. This is true
whether his system is manual or going to EDP. This
rate of change is also induced by (a) the increasing
availability of (1) both a wide variety of business ma-

chines and (2) more sophisticated machines and communications systems; and by (b) the 'systems concept' approach to the solution of business problems.

"2. A basic problem is that *intra-company* compatibility takes distinct precedence over *inter-company* compatibility. In fact, *intra-company* is the sole view generally.

What is needed?

"I. Common languages that are common to all modes and all shippers for places (origins and destinations) and for commodities.

"II. EDP updating of—at least the simpler—tariffs; so that shippers can buy low-cost punched cards or magnetic tape to avert high initial key-punching charges.

"III. Nationwide methods of uniform duplication of bills of lading into waybills and freight bills.

"The common language for place names should have the following characteristics:

Be a unique number for each specific pier, siding, municipality, etc.

Have a logical sequence to perform one or more of the following functions:

Automatically identify state and country.

Have a grid characteristic for mathematical solution of distribution problems.

Fulfill the additional maximum number of shipper, carrier and governmental agency roles.

Be looked upon as 'Esperanto' that will not necessarily be used, per se, in companies or the government but can be used by machine translation between varying machine languages.

"The common language for commodities apparently should be a digital number that would replace the item number in rail, motor, etc., classifications, and preferably fulfill I.C.C. statistical requirements from the carriers but still be related to the

Standard Industrial Code of the Bureau of Census for reporting the nation's production of goods and services."[7]

Computerizing present-day "paperwork"

Use of electronic memory storage and data processing computers will eventually make possible elimination of much of the
mass of "paperwork" that now flows alongside the physical
freight shipment. Accomplishment requires application of
simple markings that will permit self-identification of railroad
freight cars, also trucks, trailers and containers as they pass
beside sensing devices. This identification will take the place
of the waybill. It will be the "passing report," since it can be
transmitted electrically into as many computer centers as are
interested and are, at the moment, linked together. The complete procedure might be somewhat as follows, using a freight
car as example.

When the freight car is loaded, its number, lading and consignee will go to the shipper's, railroad's, and receiver's computers simultaneously. From then on, the freight car number
will control the physical movement. Each time it passes a track-
side sensing device, its location will become a new fact as to its
progress. Before it reaches each classification yard, the computer serving the local yard personnel will have linked its number, its gross weight, nature of its contents and its destination.
This will result in selection of the proper track to which the
car will be "humped" into position in the selected outgoing
train. As the train leaves the yard, presence of the correct cars
will be checked again by the computer and the next yard, and
the receiver notified as to progress toward them.

Approaching its final destination, the car number will again
pick up within the railroad computer all needed information as
to the freight bill to be rendered. The freight bill will be origi-
nated as a punched card in the railroad office; its duplicate will
simultaneously be reproduced by the computer in the receiver's
office. On receipt of proof that the car has arrived and has been
unloaded, the receiver will add to this freight bill any notations
as to damage sustained en route, at the same time informing

---

[7] *Ibid.,* see Note 6.

the railroad computer. The freight bill form will then become the basis for customer payment by being mailed to a regional or national freight bill clearinghouse. Here it will become part of the final steps of proof of customer payment, post-audit of the transaction, payment of each carrier, settlement of claims, carrier accounting and assembly of statistical data for regulatory agencies.

The present "paperwork" procedures were modern and efficient long steps forward when worked out and installed decades ago. Today they are absolute. There are too many copies of too many forms. There are numerous chances for errors to creep in. Often the "paperwork" is slow and actually delays the physical movement until the papers catch up with the car.

Placing the freight rates and the related facts as to particular freight movements in computers will simplify and speed up common carrier transportation. There is no valid reason for continuing the present complexities and annoyances inherent in today's procedures, mountains of paperwork and trillions of unused freight rates in regulatory agency files.

The need or demand for freight transportation fluctuates daily, weekly and seasonally, and also reflects long-time growth or decline in business activity. What looks like elasticity of demand actually is cross-elasticity. It is the transfer of traffic from one carrier or mode to another. Much "buyer's market" leverage has been devoted by users to forcing down the prices paid for freight transportation by playing one carrier or mode against another. Such tactics may reduce particular freight rates, but do not reduce the cost of transportation. Viewed as a whole, freight rates can be substantially reduced only by carrier-user cooperative actions that convert volume into efficiency rather than congestion, that reduce inherent excess capacity by optimum equipment utilization, and that reduce or eliminate physical and paperwork annoyances which encourage private carriage.

Chapter VIII

RELATIONSHIP OF DEFENSE
TRANSPORTATION LOGISTICS
TO BUSINESS LOGISTICS

Mechanized modes of transportation have become a major logistical factor in modern warfare, both in the combat area and behind it. The first notable beginnings in military and industrial use of railroads and steam-powered vessels occurred during the American War Between the States. Since then defense transportation decisions have had increasing impact upon the would-be civilian user of transportation in each succeeding war emergency. For example, when production of military tanks became a vital need in World War II, one effect was suspension of civilian truck production. This directly affected both carriers by truck and users of trucks, as well as the railroads which had to transport what would otherwise have been shipped by the unproduced trucks.

Business logisticians have tended to take an interest in the impact of defense transportation planning and decision-making only when our nation was actually at war. However, it is then too late to make adjustments that might have been possible if worked out earlier. The user or carrier may complain but the government can and often must issue an order. The user or carrier must then obey, even if his own optimum logistical plan is thereby upset. It follows that cooperative study and planning by business and defense logisticians can and should be carried out in peacetime. The goal of cooperation would be to have less confusion. The result will be greater effectiveness for defense transportation measures when and where they are required.

The success of defense transportation decisions and actions depends upon their nature and upon the willing acceptance of those directly affected. Both world wars have been proving grounds. Hence one might expect the nature of the needed decisions and orders to be well established. This is not the case because of the great changes that have been taking place in transportation, especially the increase in private carriage, and the strides made in commercial aviation. Even greater reliance must in the future be placed on the willing and effective co-operation of carriers and users. The following excerpts from a survey made by the author in 1944 show that even then cooperative effort was of prime importance.

Defense transportation in March, 1944, during
World War II

"American transportation has chalked up hundreds of new records in the course of providing for the requirements of World War II. The railroads particularly are astonished at their own ability to absorb the shock of war. Their performance is equivalent to all the work done by America's railroads in 1918 at the height of World War I plus all of the transportation effort of 1939, which was itself a record-breaking year in many respects. This performance has been turned out with 22,000 fewer passenger cars and 600,000 fewer freight cars than the railroads had in 1918.

"British rail carriers are also establishing new performance records. The heaviest traffic density of any railroads the world over has been maintained and exceeded in spite of the destruction and annoyance caused by more than 10,000 separate air attacks. Their average freight train is loaded 25% heavier than in 1939. British passenger trains are being cancelled without notice, diners have been taken out of service, and the number of trains available for civilian use has been drastically curtailed.

"In the United States a large portion of both passenger coaches and pullman cars is being operated exclusively for the purpose of carrying military personnel. In addition, regular trains are used to a very large extent by soldiers and sailors on furlough or in small groups. No extra train service is permitted in the United States beyond established runs. When special military movements occur, as for example for the evacuation of wounded brought by ship to a port, trains are requisitioned by the military authorities regardless of the effect upon passenger reservations and civilian travel plans. A national campaign to lessen the passenger travel burden is beginning to have some effect. Government employees are not permitted to take vacations during heavy travel periods, such as the Christmas holidays. Conventions have been curtailed. Vacation travel may be lessened as the unpleasant experiences of those returning from Florida this spring become more widely known by civilians.

The effect of manpower shortages

"Manpower shortages constitute the principal reason why American transportation has not been able to expand to meet all problems. In February, 1944, sixty-four of America's railroads reported that a total of more than 1,000 trains had been delayed one hour or more waiting for crews. These same railroads reported that approximately 2,000 switching tricks had not been worked for lack of crews. Clearly, those who travel can consider themselves fortunate in being able to obtain comfortable cars, clean pullman beds and good meals. When these comforts are curtailed travellers should remember that in other countries around the world passengers count themselves fortunate to be able to carry enough food and to have a sufficiently warm blanket or rug to offset the delays and the stern reality of unheated passenger space.

"It is scarcely necessary to add that the manpower situation has had a drastic effect in the United States upon motor transportation. First, the lack of manpower to go all the way around resulted in suspension of production of passenger automobiles and of most trucks intended for civilian use. Second, a shortage of repair parts and of repair materials such as rubber has become a familiar problem. Only the most important needs could justify diversion of manpower, as for example into the construction of artificial rubber producing factories. Third, drafting of young men hit motor transportation with great force as it took away truck drivers, bus drivers, repair mechanics and service station employees by the tens of thousands.

Effective teamwork is the key

"The miracle that has enabled America to meet essential transportation needs throughout World War II at unprecedented levels is cooperation and organization. The government, the railroads, truck carriers and shippers have been working together in an unusually effective team. Their joint efforts have carried us to this point in World War II without any breakdown or congestion or embargo comparable to the terrible difficulties of World War I. In other words, the lessons of 1917 and 1918 were well learned and have resulted in sufficient rail and truck transportation being available throughout the United States to whatever extent it was really needed. The following simple but vital rules of shipper-carrier cooperation have proven effective:

1. Load and unload freight cars and trucks promptly.
2. Keep freight cars and trucks in motion, not standing idle.
3. Organize and use freight consolidating plans for both less than truckload and less than carload.
4. Avoid and reduce civilian passenger travel.
5. Stockpile needed materials, particularly coal.
6. Load and pack and unload freight so as to avoid damage to material which will require transportation of a replacement.
7. Load cars and trucks to capacity."[1]

WORLD WAR II ORGANIZATION AND RECENT DEVELOPMENTS

During World War II improved organizations were set up for transportation control, particularly the Office of Defense Transportation directed by Joseph B. Eastman. These agencies avoided and minimized the need for supplementation of

---

[1] E. G. Plowman, Goodfellows Club, Pittsburgh, March 1944. Mimeographed.

control measures by means of government operation, as had happened during World War I. Under Director Eastman ODT placed major reliance on effective voluntary cooperation by shippers and carriers. Carrier associations were given important responsibilities. For example, the Association of American Railroads was made responsible for meeting specific military freight and passenger requirements. It was able to do so with minimum dislocation of normal and needed service to defense industry and to the general public. After the war, the Office of Defense Transportation was eventually terminated. However a similar agency, the Defense Transportation Administration, came into existence in 1950 to oversee domestic transportation during the Korean War period. It was terminated in 1955.

ODT and DTA were limited in their control powers to the modes of transportation regulated by the Interstate Commerce Commission, particularly railroads, highway, and inland waterway barge. The need for coordination within the government, including the ocean vessel and air transportation modes was only partially met by means of an inter-agency committee. However, ODT was able to keep the ports clear of excessive congestion by its planned and scheduled arrangement of movement-for-export.

In 1950 the Department of Defense established internal agencies with peacetime and wartime responsibility for transportation planning and movement control. In 1962 a similar coordinating activity was established on the civilian side of the government, to come into being in event of an emergency.

The following excerpts from President Kennedy's May 26, 1961, special message to Congress emphatically point out the need for integrating civil defense into our national defense. He stated that:

"One major element of the national security program which this Nation has never squarely faced up to is civil defense. This problem arises not from present trends but from past inaction. In the past decade we have intermittently considered a variety of programs, but we have never adopted a consistent policy. Public considerations have been largely characterized by apathy, indifference and skepticism; while, at the same time, many of the civil defense plans proposed have been so far-reaching or unrealistic that they have not gained essential support."

Recent emergency transportation organization developments

President Kennedy has followed these constructively critical comments of May 1961 with actions that have completely reorganized civil defense in all its aspects, including the vital area of defense transportation. By means of more than a dozen executive orders the planning and operation tasks have been delegated to appropriate agencies within the government. The White House announcement dated February 17, 1962, outlines what had been done up to that time, as follows:

"Steps previously taken include the transfer of major civil defense responsibilities to the Secretary of Defense by Executive Order 10952 of July 20, 1961, the assignment of emergency food and medical stockpiling responsibilities to the Secretaries of Agriculture, and Health, Education, and Welfare by Executive Order 10958 of August 14, 1961, and the reconstitution of the former Office of Civil and Defense Mobilization (OCDM) as a small Presidential staff agency under the new title of Office of Emergency Planning (OEP)."

The announcement continued—

"The President [on February 16, 1962] signed nine [additional] Executive Orders assigning emergency preparedness functions to the Secretaries of the Interior, Agriculture, Commerce, Labor, and Health, Education, and Welfare, to the Postmaster General, to the Administrator of the Federal Aviation Agency, to the Housing and Home Finance Administrator and to the Interstate Commerce Commission. These orders direct the agencies to undertake plans and programs in their areas of responsibility. . . . For example, the Secretary of Commerce will develop plans for the control and allocation of transportation in an emergency."

The Secretary of Commerce, in Executive Order 10999, one of the nine referred to in President Kennedy's press release, has received by delegation and by emphasis important tasks and powers. Of great importance is his new task of developing short- and long-time estimates of emergency requirements for commercial transportation, both military and civilian, and comparing these requirements with estimates of capability under emergency conditions. This survey will reveal existing gaps due either to unbalanced or deficiency situations. The order also states that, where necessary, he is to initiate actions or recommendations to improve the "peacetime structure of the transportation system for use in an emergency."

Other important guide-lines from Executive Order 10999 of February 16, 1962, are as follows:

"[It provides for] centralized control of all modes of transportation in an emergency . . . [and instructs the Secretary of Commerce to] develop plans . . . and be prepared to provide the necessary administrative facilities. . . .

"[It calls for] programs designed to integrate the mobilization requirements for movement of all forms of commerce with all forms of national and international transportation systems including air, ground, water and pipelines, in an emergency, [such] plans and procedures [to be developed] in consonance with international treaties and in cooperation with other Federal agencies.

"[The Executive Order states that there must be] proper apportionment and allocation of the total civil transportation capacity, or any portion thereof, to meet over-all essential civil and military needs, [utilizing] to the maximum those capabilities of other agencies qualified to perform or assist—by contractual or other agreements."

The purpose of this group of Executive Orders is, in addition to providing permanent organization for coordination, to make sure that each agency within the Federal Government has its specific area of authority. For example, the Interstate Commerce Commission is assigned full responsibility for preparing national emergency plans and for development of programs covering utilization, control and operation of interstate domestic surface transportation in an emergency. Thus ICC has been given the same role as when the Office of Defense Transportation (ODT—later DTA) was in existence during World War II and the Korean War.

The Executive Orders specifically withhold any authority "to put into effect any emergency plan, procedure, policy, program or course of action prepared or developed pursuant to this order. Such authority is reserved to the President. . . . The Director of the Office of Emergency Planning (OEP) shall advise and assist the President in determining policy for, and assist him in coordinating the performance of functions under this order with the total national preparedness program."

The interrelations within and between these Executive Orders are very numerous. To detail them would be tedious— and would lead to a false impression of confusion. The fact is that the orders have greatly increased the possibility of effective and coordinated control of America's transportation under emergency conditions caused by enemy action.

Pursuant to Executive Order 10999, there has been established within the Department of Commerce an Office of Emergency Transportation (OET) under the direction of the Under Secretary of Commerce for Transportation. If and when the President finds that emergency conditions so require, this OET agency will be ready. As Executive Order 10999 succinctly puts it, the "Secretary [of Commerce] shall be prepared to implement all appropriate plans developed under this order. Modifications and temporary organizational changes, based on emergency conditions, will be in accordance with policy determination by the President." These provisions as to organizational changes will govern conversion of the peacetime OET into the wartime agency. To visualize this transition, the problem at that time will be to convert a small peacetime agency into a larger and nation-wide transportation coordinating activity.

Importance of the executive reserve

The Office of Emergency Transportation will be ready to become the nucleus of an expanded wartime agency whenever so needed because it consists, in peacetime, of a small, permanent staff and a relatively large group of "executive reservists" who have worked together. The entire team, consisting of the peacetime nucleus and the executive reservists, must be ready and competent to operate in time of emergency on both a national and regional level.

Existence and operation of the emergency transportation agency is necessary, for example, to avoid the possible segmentation of transportation in an emergency. To do this there must be development of state and local coordination in performance of transportation control duties belonging to the intrastate level of government.

The Executive Reserve is the skilled group that would move into Federal offices at both the national and regional levels to help cope with transportation problems arising due to emergency conditions caused by enemy action. Reservists have generally agreed to take time from their daily responsibilities for periodic training and to stand ready to participate full-time in the event of an emergency.

The Executive Reserve Program of the Federal Maritime Administration is described in detail as an example of what is being done. A very similar and effective program has been developed by the Interstate Commerce Commission.

"Maritime will invite qualified persons to participate in the programs. These persons will be selected largely from former Maritime employees and executives of the Marine and port operations industry.

"Each Reservist will be asked to submit a statement of understanding containing:

"(1) A statement of the Reservist's willingness to attend a course of training at least once a year at Washington or regional points when possible.

"(2) A statement of the Reservist's immediate availability for assignment in the event of a national emergency, barring unforeseen and overriding reasons to the contrary;

"(3) The concurrence in (1) and (2) above of the Reservist's private employer, or in the case of a government employee, of a responsible official of his agency.

"(4) A statement that the Reservist will notify the designating department or agency when his employment or personal status changes in such a manner as to make it unlikely that he would be available for full-time service in the event of a national emergency.

"Candidates must be cleared for security. . . . Fingerprinting is included. This is necessary in order to have the security requirements completed in advance of any emergency. Also Reservists may be furnished classified information from time to time as part of their training.

"Reserve service is wholly on a voluntary basis and reserve status may be terminated at any time at the discretion of the Reservist or his employer."

TRANSPORTATION UNDER FUTURE EMERGENCY CONDITIONS

The surplus transportation capacity that could be called upon in past wars was almost entirely concentrated in common carriers. It consisted in the better use of railroads, the better scheduling and use of common carrier trucks, barges, pipelines, vessels and aircraft. It was essentially and chiefly a common carrier surplus. Today, the surplus of transportation capability exists also and perhaps largely in the form of privately owned barges and towboats or ships, and privately owned aircraft.

Another change that has taken place since World War II is the greatly increased importance of commercial aviation. Air navigation and airport control will presumably be under military direction. In a shooting war, with the shooting here, military authorities must be the ones to decide when and where non-military aircraft can go into the air.

An important and growing segment of defense transportation is owned, operated or controlled by our government, using that term to include not only the Army, the Navy, the Air Force and the Marine Corps but also the civilian branches of the Federal government as well as our state and local governmental agencies. Among the different kinds of transportation owned by government that have potential defense transportation usefulness, a few examples may serve as reminder of both quantity and variety:

There are a number of government-owned cargo vessels operated by the Military Sea Transportation Service, and there are many more in the laid-up fleet.

There are a number of government-owned passenger and cargo airplanes operated by the Military Air Transportation Service.

There are thousands of radio-equipped patrol automobiles owned and operated by municipal and state governments.

There are thousands of trucks owned and operated by the Post Office and other civilian federal agencies. There is also a sizeable inventory of military trucks and buses.

The paved streets of our urban areas, the paved rural highways and the new super highways are an integral part of our defense transportation system. Plans must be made for their repair and maintenance, as well as their safety signalling and patrol, under emergency conditions.

There are many other government-owned facilities and reserves of defense transportation importance. Examples are urban bus and subway transportation systems, the locks and dredged channels of rivers and harbors, the nation's airways and airports, helicopters that may be equipped for military or rescue missions, and amphibious vehicles capable of traveling on water or snow or land.

The need for mobilizing transportation for defense

Despite the wide variety and large quantity of government-owned defense transportation, the United States must also mobilize the vast civilian transportation resources. The total amount and variety owned and operated by common carriers, contract carriers, so-called exempt carriers and private persons and enterprises for their own purposes is greater than the government reserves just described. In addition, government and private enterprise transportation activities interlock in so many ways that often one is valueless without the other. Thus bus and truck operations depend on the public streets and highways; operators of vessels and barges require government-maintained harbors, dredged channels and aids to navigation, such as lighthouses; airplanes must have municipal airports, air lanes and flight control.

The increasing size of the private transportation segment is a new factor that may in the future lessen the effectiveness of emergency transportation plans. By private operation is meant the millions of private automobiles and the tens of thousands of trucks operated by farmer and business enterprises for their own purposes, also the thousands of privately owned and operated aircraft and shallow-draft vessels. Private transportation since World War II has grown both in amount and ratio faster than has common carriage.

As these unequal growth rates continue, there is relatively less and less defense transportation that can be secured from the for-hire segment. It follows that in a future war some of the requirements for defense transportation may have to be obtained from the private transportation sector. This possibility emphasizes the point that effective and successful national defense transportation requires use, to whatever extent is required, of any or all of the transportation capability, whether government-owned, for-hire or private in character. The relation to and effect upon business logistics thus will become more and more direct.

Top priority must be given to the furnishing of whatever direct military transportation is required. This task has been accomplished in the past and particularly with great effectiveness in World War II, primarily by the willing efforts of common carriers. It will be accomplished in any future war, but common carriers may not have the capacity to do the job.

Civil defense authorities have the right and duty to control all transportation within any area that has suffered damage from enemy action. Civil defense control of transportation within a bomb-damaged area is full of complications that have been publicly debated in newspapers and in government publicity. There will be the urgent problem of sustaining the war effort by providing or restoring the interstate transportation required by defense production. There will be both interstate and local transportation requirements for medicine, food, clothing, gasoline and maintenance-type supplies such as tires, batteries and window glass for the civilian population.

Anyone who believes that, in any future war emergency, these priorities will automatically adjust themselves is naive. Even if perfect coordination exists at the federal, state, and local government levels and between these levels, there can be no assurance that any preconceived plans will fit the facts of the actual emergency. It seems certain that, despite the variety and immense reserves inherent in present-day government-owned and civilian-owned for-hire equipment, also in private operation, over-all inadequacies and spot shortages will characterize the next major war in which the United States is directly involved.

The emergency highway control problem

Business logistics decisions are arrived at by the use of mathematical analysis of a complex array of facts as to production problems, packaging and warehousing alternatives, customer requirements and related transportation movements. Similarly, defense transportation is involved in and part of military logistics decision making. Defense transportation decisions cannot be automatically coordinated with business logistics decisions within a computer. As has been shown, the interaction between them is becoming more frequent and of greater impact in wartime and even in so-called "cold war" situations. Hence business logisticians need to understand the problems of defense transportation in order to cooperate and to minimize adverse impacts.

Emergency highway control exemplifies the increased interrelation of defense transportation and business logistics. The problem to be solved is how to apportion the use of a community asset, that is, a particular inter-city highway, when the desire to travel over it exceeds its capacity. Assume that a highway fifty miles long connecting cities located in two different states has a normal capacity of 1,000 vehicles per hour in each direction. Further assume that it has been damaged so that at its "choke points" its capacity has been reduced to 1,000 vehicles per hour in one direction only. Finally assume that the intercity demands will exceed the 1,000 vehicles per hour total capacity of the highway. In addition, unless prevented from doing so, short distance local traffic will use the road in both directions.

The assumed conditions show the need for effective control of the particular highways. This control must be of coordinated nature. Local authorities, state police, the highway departments of the two states, associations of highway users, the civilian and military authorities of the Federal government, all must work together.

Absence of any control could result in use of all of the available capacity by vehicles that have low rather than the highest priority. Or it can result in clogging the highway with wrecked vehicles or with vehicles trying to move in opposite directions where there is only a single lane. The purpose of coordinated control will be to avoid such happenings. Control will make it possible to use the full remaining capacity of the damaged highway for high priority purposes.

When we recall that the last important military action within the borders of the United States took place almost a century ago, we gain some appreciation of the concern of civil defense authorities as to what will be our collective behavior in the face of bombing of one or more of our cities. When we think how civil defense signs on our highways become simply an accepted part of the scenery and lose their meaning and reality to most of us, we realize how the best made plans can end in panic and in defense transportation breakdown or shortage. When we consider the difficult decisions that will have to be made during the first day of any future war, we realize how vital and necessary national defense transportation has become.

After any future major war has begun, the successful furnishing of an adequate supply of defense transportation will depend upon the quantity and quality of voluntary co-operation that can be generated. The United States is a vast country not only in area but also in population. Government orders and plans can only establish patterns. The success of defense transportation regulations will depend on millions of individual citizens. Automobile owners, truck drivers, shippers or receivers of merchandise, taxi drivers, railroad conductors and airline ticket agents must all co-operate, each in his own area. Business logisticians have a special responsibility in this cooperative effort, because their decisions and plans can provide important and needed leadership.

Chapter IX

THE LOGISTICS OF NATIONAL TRANSPORTATION POLICY

Federal transportation policy has been the outgrowth of more than a century of study and evolution. The evolutionary factors or questions of greatest importance have been as follows:

1. Should we have government or private ownership and operation of transportation? Is there a policy distinction to be made between construction of routes such as highways and operation of transportation devices such as trucks?

2. Should modes of transportation receive government assistance (called by some promotion, and by others subsidy)? Is there a policy distinction between mode improvements and government assistance given to a particular carrier?

3. Should certain kinds of transportation such as common carriers be regulated by government? Is there a policy distinction between regulation under the former so-called monopoly conditions and today's situation of competition between fully regulated, partially regulated, unregulated and private transportation?

The word "policy" has acquired a distinctive meaning in recent decades in business management. Briefly, a business policy is thought of as a basic or broad oral or written decision, arrived at by the stockholders, the board of directors or by high-level executives, and stated in general terms for the guidance of administrative levels of management.

The Federal government also uses the word "policy." It may develop its top-level policy decisions in the form of laws, or as regulatory agency findings and conclusions, or simply as oral or written directives. This variety of form can result in conflict and confusion; and such is the present situation with respect to Federal transportation policy. Thus the preamble of the Interstate Commerce Act, designated in the law as "The National Transportation Policy," is neither complete in application nor in subject matter.

Historical development of National Transportation Policy

Although there was no Federal regulatory agency, national transportation policy did develop in important ways during the first century after the American Revolution. In 1787 the Northwest Ordinance with its prohibition of tolls on inland water routes was approved by the Continental Congress. This decision was the first policy step toward present-day Federal assumption of complete responsibility for construction, improvement and maintenance of navigation facilities such as canals, channels, harbors, and lighthouses.

A procession of Federal reports on transportation began in 1808 when Albert Gallatin, then Secretary of the Treasury, sent his Transportation Report to the President and Congress. The most recent such report was the Transportation Message sent to Congress by President Kennedy in April, 1962.

The 1808 report is interesting for its prediction that railroads would have little or no future importance in America as compared to canals and roads. Gallatin advocated Federal promotion of the latter type of projects, such as the National Turnpike between Cumberland, Maryland, and Wheeling, West Virginia; and the canal connecting the Delaware River with Chesapeake Bay.

Another important early study of Federal transportation problems was personally undertaken by President James Monroe. His presidential inaugural address, on March 2, 1817, stressed the need for "improvement of our country by roads and canals, proceeding always with a constitutional sanction."

Monroe developed these views more fully during his first summer as President, spent on a long inspection trip through New England and as far west as Detroit. On December 2, 1817, he again sent a message to Congress reviewing his journey and urging the need for transportation improvements. He reiterated his view as to lack of constitutionality of expenditure of Federal funds for such interstate purposes. He stated the result of his study as "a settled conviction in my mind, that Congress does not possess the right. It is not contained in any of the specified powers granted to Congress." Having reached this negative conclusion, President Monroe went on to suggest to Congress "the propriety of recommending to the States the adoption of an amendment to the Constitution, which shall give to Congress the right in question."

President Monroe in 1822 again tried to bring about submission to the states of a constitutional amendment, at the same time vetoing an appropriation for much-needed repair and improvement of the then 10-year-old National Turnpike between Cumberland and the Ohio River at Wheeling. The resulting political storm caused him to reverse his position. In his message to Congress on December 3, 1822, Monroe accepted refusal of that body to propose an amendment as its verdict on the question of constitutionality. He requested the appropriation for the dusty turnpike's repairs, and the Congress promptly complied. Thus Congress in its action in 1822 established an important element in today's national transportation policy, namely national responsibility for promotion of means of highway transportation between the states.

Present-day national transportation policy in the regulatory area is largely the product of the two decades after 1865. Mounting criticism against the political and economic policies and practices of railroads and large shippers culminated in establishment of the Interstate Commerce Commission in 1887. Decision to establish this regulatory agency created another element or factor in national transportation policy.

Before 1910 the modern paved interstate highway was still an unlikely dream. The concept of multipurpose river development (drinking water, water for industrial use, water for recreation, coupled with flood control and man-made navigable channels) was likewise only being dreamed and talked about. More and more stringent Federal regulation of the only nation-wide type of common carrier, the railroads, seemed then to be the major national policy problem. All this began to change after World War I.

For a few years, nationalization of common carriers seemed about to become embedded in national policy. This came about because, after World War I, the Federal government found itself the operator of the nation's railroads, also of the only large-scale commercial barge line on the Mississippi River, and of most of the ocean-going vessels then operating to and from U.S. ports.

Congress in 1919 turned back the operation of the railroads to their owners. In 1936 Congress passed an act that confirmed the placing of responsibility for operation of ocean-going vessels in private enterprise hands. In 1953 the government sold its inland waterway barge operation. Each of these actions stemmed in part from congressional hearings and in part from reports prepared by the government. For example, the decision to sell the river barge enterprise to a private operator was urged in the first Hoover Commission Report. This turning away from government operation of railroads, ocean vessels and barges thus became another important element in present-day national transportation policy.

RECENT LEGISLATIVE STATEMENTS AS TO NATIONAL TRANSPORTATION POLICY

After World War I Congress made its first statement as to national transportation policy in the preamble of the Transportation Act of 1920. This preamble emphasized public interest in development of inland waterway transportation as a full partner with and competitor of rail transportation. It did not mention pipelines which had been placed under ICC regulation in 1906. Perhaps this was because lengthy Supreme Court litigation was not settled until 1920. The preamble stated that:

"It is hereby declared to be the policy of Congress to promote, encourage and develop water transportation, service
and facilities in connection with the commerce of the United
States, and to foster and preserve in full vigor both rail
and water transportation."

In 1925, Congress experimented with legislative freight
rate making by passing the Hoch-Smith Resolution in which:

"It is hereby declared to be the true policy in rate making
to be pursued by the Interstate Commerce Commission in
adjusting freight rates, that the conditions which at any
time prevail in our several industries should be considered,
insofar as it is legally possible to do so, to the end that commodities may freely move."

Perhaps Congress was thinking of its fostering attitude
toward inland waterway barge transportation, or possibly
the Canadian Crow's Nest Pass Agreement was its inspira-
tion. This Canadian example of what government should not
do has resulted in maintenance on grain and grain products
eastbound from their prairie provinces, of freight rates unchanged in amount since the agreement date of 1897.

Although the Hoch-Smith Resolution never was repealed,
the trend away from legislative freight rate making is, happily,
unmistakable. When the government sold its inland waterway
barge operation it abandoned any possible usage of this instru-
mentality for making so-called "yardstick freight rates." Congress also has repealed the land-grant freight rate concessions,
leaving only the so-called Section 22 provisions. These latter
are often criticized by business users of transportation. Government, in its role as shipper, is claimed by some critics to be
able to use this exemption from regulatory control to exact an
unfairly low freight rate from an over eager common or contract carrier.

In 1935 the Motor Carrier Act was passed. Its preamble
declared it to be:

"The policy of Congress to regulate transportation by
motor vehicle in such manner as to recognize and preserve
the inherent advantages, improve the relations between

and coordinate transportation by motor carriers and other carriers, develop and preserve a highway transportation system."

This 1935 declaration of policy thus recognized the importance of a fourth mode of transportation within the United States. Clearly Congress had become interested in the welfare and the regulation of all means of common carrier transportation. In rapid succession Congress added new legislation with respect to ocean merchant vessel transportation and commercial air transportation, the first in 1936 and the second in 1938. Congress declared in the Merchant Marine Act of 1936 that,

"It is hereby declared to be the policy of the United States to foster the development and encourage the maintenance of a merchant marine sufficient to carry the domestic waterborne commerce and a substantial portion of the waterborne export and import foreign commerce, capable of service as a naval and military auxiliary in time of war and constructed in the United States."

In the Civil Aeronautics Act of 1938, Congress did not use the word "policy," but the now-familiar elements are spelled out as instructions to the Civil Aeronautics Board, as follows:

"The encouragement and development of an air transportation system properly adapted to the present and future needs of the foreign and domestic commerce—regulation in such manner as to recognize and preserve the inherent advantages—promotion of adequate, economical and efficient service by air carriers."

The Transportation Act of 1940 Policy Preamble

In 1940, the first and so far the only step toward a consolidated statement of transportation policy was taken by Congress. In the Transportation Act of 1940, which deals only with the regulatory responsibilities of the Interstate Commerce Commission, Congress stated:

"It is hereby declared to be the National Transportation Policy of the Congress to provide for fair and impartial regulation of all modes of transportation subject to the provisions of this Act, so administered as to recognize and preserve the inherent advantages of each—all to the end of developing, coordinating and preserving a national transportation system by water, highway and rail, as well as other means, adequate to meet the needs of the commerce of the United States, of the Postal Service and of the national defense."

This is the first use by Congress of the expression "National Transportation Policy." The language does not limit the policy to carriers using the inland waterways, interstate highways and railroad routes, but includes other means as well. Certainly pipelines and freight forwarders and coastwise and Great Lakes vessel transportation would be encompassed to the extent that they are regulated by the Interstate Commerce Commission. This broad statement, supplemented by the similar statements in the Merchant Marine Act of 1936 and in the Civil Aeronautics Act of 1938, does indeed constitute a general and high-level government decision as to National Transportation Policy. By the terms of this Policy, Congress desires to encourage and develop each and every means or mode of transportation, recognizing and preserving the inherent advantages of each, and coordinating all carriers into a national transportation system.

The second Hoover Commission, in its March 1955 report on administration of Federal traffic management, referred to confusion it had found within the government as to these points. It urged that the National Transportation Policy portion of the Interstate Commerce Act be restated more clearly by Congress and, in such revised form, be accepted and followed by all Federal officials. An obvious alternative to this suggestion would be to abandon the effort to state our National Transportation Policy in general terms such as in the preamble to the Interstate Commerce Act and similar declarations in other transportation legislation.

The latest Congressional action, the Transportation Act of 1958, dealt with the wording of the preamble of the 1940 act in only one respect. In its revision of Section 15a of the 1940 act, it included the following:

"Rates of a carrier shall not be held up to a particular level to protect the traffic of any other mode of transportation, giving due consideration to the objectives of the National Transportation Policy declared in the Act."

FEDERAL TRANSPORTATION STUDIES

Since 1958, three Federal transportation studies have been added to the procession of such reports that began in 1808. These are: the 1960 Commerce study referred to as the Mueller report (Frederick Mueller, Secretary of Commerce); the 1961 Senate study referred to as the Doyle Report (John Doyle, Director of the study); and the 1962 Transportation Message to Congress referred to as President Kennedy's Transportation Message.

The 1960 Mueller report made only one specific recommendation with respect to National Transportation policy. This was restricted to the version constituting the preamble of the present Interstate Commerce Act. This proposal was to amend the policy statement "to define 'unfair and destructive competitive practices' to include only rates below the long-run marginal costs of the carrier making the rates." The purpose of this proposed change apparently was to clarify the meaning of the second part of the sentence in the 1958 revision of Section 15a of the ICC Act.

The Doyle Report

The 1961 report designated as a preliminary draft of a report prepared for the Committee on Interstate and Foreign Commerce, United States Senate, has been christened the Doyle Report after its staff director, retired Air Force Major General John P. Doyle.[1] Its title and purpose is to review and make recommendations as to evolution and improvement of

[1] Eighty-seventh Congress, First Session, National Transportation Policy, Jan. 3, 1961, U.S. Government Printing Office, Washington, D.C.

National Transportation Policy. In a section headed by the subtitle, Conclusions, we read the following:

"Technology, uncoordinated and expanding public aid, shipper bias in favor of maximizing competition and certain regulatory policies have together brought about an excessive number of carriers and overexpansion of transportation plant. They have set up trends which if continued unabated to 1975, will see private carriage rather than common carriage the base of the nation's transportation system. The railroads, unable to adjust expenses to declining volume of business, may become government owned. This nation will not permit the railroads to go by the board and properly so. Common carriers as we have known them are disappearing in water transportation and the highway common carriers are losing relative position and facing a prospect of higher operating ratios. The social investment per ton-mile and passenger-mile will in transportation increase with the continued decline of common carriers. It is doubtful if the growing mass transportation requirements between major centers of the nation can be adequately served at any cost by private and contract carrier operations."[2]

The Doyle Report also presented suggestions for improved organization of Federal and regulatory and promotional activities.

"The Civil Aeronautics Board, Interstate Commerce Commission and Federal Maritime Board should be consolidated into a single Federal Transportation Commission which would have jurisdiction over operating rights of all regulated carriers; all aspects of intra-modal rates and services, including (ocean) shipping conference agreements; approval and promulgation of safety regulations for air, highway and rail carriers; enforcement responsibility . . . and coordination of transportation research and statistical programs with the proposed Department of Transportation . . . There should be a 'strong chairman' . . . At top-staff echelons, the Commission should be organized by

2 *Ibid.,* p. 10.

purpose (such as operating rights, rates, and services, etc.) for all modes, to avoid top-level organization by clientele (rail, air, highway, waterway and pipeline) . . ."[3]

The report goes on to recommend a Department of Transportation with four major areas of promotional activity described as follows:

"(a) Certain existing agencies and the transport programs they administer. These include the Bureau of Public Roads, Defense Air Transportation Administration, Federal Aviation Agency, Maritime Administration, Office of Under Secretary of Commerce for Transportation, Panama Canal Company, [and the] St. Lawrence Seaway Development Corporation . . .

"(b) Responsibility . . . for policy formation, policy review and surveillance . . . [of such non-transferable agencies as the] traffic management functions of the General Services Administration, Department of Defense, and Post Office . . .; planning and administration of rivers and harbors work of Corps of Engineers; Tennessee Valley Authority functions related to navigation; and . . . mapping and weather reporting.

"(c) Transfer to it of certain executive type functions currently being performed by [regulatory agencies] such as [field] enforcement . . . airmail subsidy program . . . merchant marine subsidies, and [railroad and other] guaranteed loan programs.

"(e) Establishment of executive leadership . . . [such as by] promoting technological advances in all modes . . . formation of broad transport policy supported by research . . . [and] providing needed transportation services during national or regional emergencies . . ."[4]

The Doyle Report emphasizes the importance of urban commutation as a railroad problem as follows:

"Rail commutation revenues have seldom recovered the cost of the service and the deficits have been made up from

---

[3] *Ibid.*, p. 11.
[4] *Ibid.*, pp. 11–12.

freight profits. . . . It is no longer possible to force freight shippers to subsidize commuters. . . . Enough alternative commuter transportation exists to reduce the proceeds from fare increases due to the number of riders lost with each increase.[5]

Merger of railroads is also urged as important. The Doyle Report urged that:

"General consolidation of railroads in the near future is presented as the most important measure to restore the railroad industry to the health and vigorous status of over 30 years ago and as a necessary basis for a coordinated transportation system for the nation. . . . The public interest in maintaining privately owned railroads as a basic element of an efficient transportation system and one that will provide for economic growth and national defense requires early action. . . . The public interest requires a regional or national approach beginning with the northeast area where conditions of the [railroad] industry are acute."[6]

PRESIDENT KENNEDY'S TRANSPORTATION MESSAGE

President Kennedy's Message to Congress on Transportation, dated April 5, 1962, is the newest and the most significant of the three recent Federal reports. Unlike the 1960 study, the Transportation Message offers no suggested changes in wording of the policy preambles of the ICC, CAB and Maritime legislation. Unlike the 1961 report, the Transportation Message does not make broad reorganization proposals. This 1962 President's Message on Transportation is unique in its orientation toward actions rather than toward more wordy discussion. This comes from its being a Presidential message. In addition its arrangement of subjects and its approach is specific rather than theoretical. There is recognition that much can and should be done without new legislation. Its discussion of subjects aims at action—at doing now what can be done.

---

[5] *Ibid.,* p. 581.
[6] *Ibid.,* pp. 15–16.

The 1962 message discusses approximately 50 specific subjects. About 20 are instructions or suggestions that do not require new legislation. There are about 30 recommendations for Congress to consider. Many of the 50 proposals affect National Transportation Policy.

President Kennedy used his Message to create a number of organizational improvements within the government. Thus he asked the Secretary of Commerce and the Housing and Home Finance Administrator to consult together and to report to the President annually as to coordination of highway and mass transportation activities in urban areas. He also recommended that final approval of urban highways be conditioned upon a finding that the project is consistent with comprehensive development plans for the particular metropolitan area. This important addition to National Transportation Policy was enacted into law in 1962 by Congress, to become effective in 1965.

Another step forward taken by President Kennedy in his 1962 Message was in recognition of the vital importance to national transportation policy of research and development. His instructions to government agencies in the Message were:

1. Recognition of the Department of Commerce as the Federal agency to make broad evaluations of transportation problems and to undertake a comprehensive research program.

2. Creation of a Cabinet level committee to study maritime "flags of convenience" and "cargo preference" issues, and recommendation of a stepped-up research program aimed at increasing the competitive efficiency of the merchant marine.

3. Creation of an interagency group to assist the Department of Justice in developing the government's position in transportation merger cases for presentation before the appropriate regulatory agency.

4. Encouragement of Department of Defense and General Services Administration exploration and experimentation aimed at developing improved rates and services and simplified rate structures.

5. Endorsement of the Department of Commerce Census Bureau proposal for a Census of Transportation, aimed especially at filling gaps in such areas as private carriage of freight.

6. The President also urged Congress to increase the percentage of Federal highway funds available for state research and development projects, and asked that the fund provided by Congress for urban mass transportation grants be broadened into a research and development program in this area.

The 1962 Message to Congress made numerous recommendations for changes in transportation laws. The most important of these suggestions would implement, in various detailed ways, the clearly stated national transportation policy of equality of Federal treatment of each of the modes coupled with reduction in the scope of Federal regulation. This policy was also stated in the Message as greater reliance on competition between modes and carriers and less reliance upon the Federal government as umpire and as the source of financial assistance. The Message made the following recommendations:

1. Urged Congress to enact legislation eliminating existing regulatory agency authority to prescribe minimum rates on bulk commodities, agricultural and fishery products, or alternatively, to eliminate the existing bulk and agriculture exemptions by barge and highway.

2. Urged legislation to assure all carriers the right to ship vehicles or containers on carriers of other branches of the transportation industry at the same rates available to non-carrier shippers.

3. Urged Congress to declare as a matter of public policy that through routes and joint rates between carriers of the same or different modes should be brought about.

4. Recommended an equitable system of user charges for aviation and extension of the principle of user charges to inland waterways. The President also pointed out the importance of reducing the payment of subsidies for encouragement of aviation.

5. The President pointed out the importance of steps to reduce the so-called "gray area" of private trucking. He urged legislation to give the Interstate Commerce Commission authority to enter into cooperative enforcement agreements with the various states, and suggested increase in the penalties levied for violation of highway safety regulations.

6. The Message also proposed legislation to permit Federal grants and other assistance to mass transportation of commuter type.

INTERRELATION OF NATIONAL TRANSPORTATION POLICY AND BUSINESS LOGISTICS

Business executives, including traffic and packaging and warehouse managers, tend to minimize the importance of National Transportation Policy. To them it is much too general a concept. Furthermore, as has been shown, it is inadequately written out and therefore is subject to change and evolution. These criticisms have only slight validity. They are very wide of the mark. They overlook the fact that active competition among carriers and freedom of choice by users, including use of private carriage, have been made possible by the policies adopted and followed by the Federal government. For example, if the railroads in 1920 had remained in government control, Federal policy toward construction of fine highways and encouragement of common carrier trucking might not have become established. It would have been tempting to the government, as has been done in some foreign countries, to try to force trucking into a short-haul collection and distribution role. This could have been accomplished by failure to provide adequate inter-city highways, or by prohibiting any truck from carrying freight past the nearest railroad station. Both stratagems have been used in other countries to force continued use of their nationalized railroads.

National Transportation Policy has encouraged and, to some degree, sponsored development of the modes of transportation that compete with railroads. By providing highways, barge navigation facilities, airways and airports, the Federal government has substantially broadened the variety of logistical choices. Private carriage has become a major factor. Today it is one of the most important alternative choices of business logistics, for both service and cost reduction reasons.

Government construction of better highways, better barge canals and better airports encourages private carriage by furnishing lower cost and more efficient facilities. Congestion is at least temporarily reduced so that the inherent one-way loaded, one-way empty condition of the private truck or barge or airplane is made less costly by permitting faster round trips. If private carriage is not chosen, the alternative selected often is other than common carriage. Contract carriage, including carrying of bulk and other exempt commodities, is also facilitated by the government-provided improvements.

There is a natural clash between the driver of a private automobile and the desire of an urban community to achieve reduction in traffic congestion by encouraging use of mass transportation commuter service. It is being predicted by some that this clash will ultimately result in public regulation of one's use of his own automobile. Already a somewhat similar clash exists between the support given to common carriers by existing National Transportation Policy, and the tendency of business logisticians to choose and use private carriage regardless of the effect on for-hire carriers.

Business logistics is a broad concept that includes assembly of inbound materials and distribution of finished products. Transportation is a part of this, as are also such functions as inventory planning and warehouse location. Transportation is and must be dealt with by the user as a cost, and also as a sales tool. Movements must be integrated with inventories and with location and production factors. This concept is often met most fully by private transportation. If private carriage is not feasible, the next most flexible and least costly often is contract carriage. Common carriers not only seek to make a profit, but seek to do so by serving as part of the logistics pattern of many customers. They may, however, lack the singleness of purpose demanded by some of their customers, especially those needing flexible and tailored service.

The United States is fortunate in having competitive, low-cost transportation that provides access to every part of the 50 states for every individual and every business enterprise. This superb transportation asset is the envy of the world. However, we should not close our eyes to its internal clashes, its overcapacity and the mounting pressures against survival of its key element, common carriage. National Transportation Policy has played an important role for more than a century, both by developing the present competitive situation in transportation and by causing some of its greatest problems. Thorough understanding of and effective support for revision and improvement of National Transportation Policy should be a major concern of business logistics.

INDEX

TRANSPORTATION AS A NATIONAL SYSTEM